THE ESSENTIAL
MURIEL RUKEYSER

THE ESSENTIAL MURIEL RUKEYSER

Poems

Selected and with an Introduction by
NATASHA TRETHEWEY

An *Imprint of* HarperCollins*Publishers*

HarperCollins books may be purchased for educational, business, or sales promotional use. For information, please email the Special Markets Department at SPsales@harpercollins.com.

FIRST EDITION

Designed by Michelle Crowe

Library of Congress Cataloging-in-Publication Data has been applied for.

ISBN 978-0-06-298549-1

21 22 23 24 25 LSC 10 9 8 7 6 5 4 3 2 1

CONTENTS

INTRODUCTION: THESE ROADS WILL TAKE YOU INTO YOUR OWN COUNTRY

by Natasha Trethewey

My earliest encounter with the poems of Muriel Rukeyser was in a seminar on contemporary American poetry in my first year of graduate school. It was 1990, she'd been dead for ten years, and as I read aloud from "The Book of the Dead"—a long sequence from Rukeyser's 1938 collection *U.S. 1*—I felt the resonant power of her living voice, and the recognition that came to me was like the lightning that accompanies a thunderclap, illuminating everything for a resounding moment:

> As dark as I am, when I came out the morning after the
>   tunnel at night,
> with a white man, nobody could have told which man was
>   white.
> The dust had covered us both, and the dust was white.

The sequence recounts the history of the industrial tragedy of the Hawk's Nest Tunnel construction project in Gauley Bridge, West Virginia. Rukeyser journeyed there to report on what had happened: industrial greed and malfeasance, the unsafe working conditions in the mines, the many deaths from silicosis (a disease that causes shortness of breath and is the result of prolonged inhalation of silica dust) that could have been prevented with proper protocols—providing masks for the workers and wet drilling. Nearly two thousand people died. The greatest percentage of the dead were African American migrant workers from the South, and in the poem's haunting image of dust (I think of the phrase *when the dust settles*), Rukeyser exposes one of the realities of race in America: the disproportionate impact of unhealthy working conditions and environmental pollutants on Black Americans. The image underscores the awful truth of history: even as the specter of death—the great leveler—shrouds them both in whiteness, one of them is more likely to die. "The poetic image is not a static thing," she wrote. "It lives in time, as does the poem." For Rukeyser, a poem's failure would be that a reader is not brought by the poem *beyond* it.

How could I not be transported by the world—that place and time—of Rukeyser's "Book of the Dead" to myriad places beyond it? She could have been writing about the Tuskegee experiment, lead in the water supply in Flint, Michigan, or the impact, across the U.S., of the COVID-19 pandemic—this moment during which, after all these years, I've turned again to her work. This is the prescience, the timeliness and timelessness of Muriel Rukeyser's poetry.

When I agreed to cull seventy-five poems from her vast body of work—to edit *The Essential Muriel Rukeyser*—it was the summer of

2019. We were not yet in the midst of a pandemic. I easily recalled that first encounter with her work as a young woman, determined to become a poet, knowing only that something about the time and place I had entered the world, and my particular circumstances, was stirring in me some great need to speak in the language of poetry. And here was a woman poet, born a half century before me, who powerfully embraced her call to bear witness, to tell what she had seen, a poet who, in the aftermath of seeing the beginning of a war, declared—when asked, *Where is there a place for poetry?*— "Then I began to say what I believe."

Her words were intoxicating, freeing, and her poems were maps into my as yet unarticulated self: "These are the roads to take when you think of your own country / and interested bring down the maps again . . . / These roads will take you into your own country . . . / Here is your road, tying / you to its meanings."

All those years ago, the introduction to her work guided me in immeasurable ways to my own thinking about poetry. I had been prepared to approach editing this volume as an admirer who would try to pull together a representative sample, its far-reaching themes, forgetting that a compilation such as this one is as much about the moment in which the editor finds herself.

By the time I finally sat down to read her collected works for this anthology, the world was in the grip of the COVID-19 pandemic, and within the social isolation of that moment, the inevitable separation of our individual lives, came the moral authority and ethical conviction of Rukeyser's voice, and I could no longer think of the idea of *essential* in the same way. As a nation, we'd been given a new way to think collectively about *what* and *who* was essential. And with the civil unrest and protests against police brutality and social injustice occurring in tandem, the idea of essential had extended to frame a national reckoning around whose lives matter, and how much; whose lives are expendable, and the many ways that the lives of Black people in this country are treated as though they matter less than lives of others. I read again and again these lines:

> What three things can never be done?
> Forget. Keep silent. Stand alone.

And:

> Pay attention to what they tell you to forget
> pay attention to what they tell you to forget
> pay attention to what they tell you to forget

I saw in them what has always been essential to me about her poems. In a nation steeped in forgetting, in many ways built upon it, Rukeyser, over the course of her long career—a life of conscientious reckoning with the self and the world—would bear witness to many of the most pressing issues of the century with the clarity and moral authority of one whose life was boldly and fully lived. Situating the origins of her poetic vision, she wrote: "War has been in my writing since I began. The first public day that I remember was the False

Armistice of 1918." That was November, in the midst of the influenza epidemic that would ultimately claim half a million U.S. lives, with a resurgence of the virus as servicemen returned from battle and precautions had lapsed at home.

It is sobering to think that day of her first public awareness was also during a pandemic, just as we are in now. And we too are contending with civil unrest, polarization, and divisiveness on a larger scale than we have seen in this nation for some time. Into moments like these a poet's work emerges that can carry us through the turbulence, a poet whose work can take you into your own country. "In time of crisis," Rukeyser wrote, "we summon up our strength."

We are in a time of crisis. Someone, somewhere, is always in a time of crisis.

Rukeyser believed in the essential role of poetry in our lives, "a type of creation in which we may live and which will save us." Save us because it is a way to feel, to communicate "a form of love." And we are a nation in need of saving; we are always in need of saving. This is what her poems offer:

> And if an essential thing has flown between us,
> rare intellectual bird of communication,
> let us seize it quickly : let our preference
> choose it instead of softer things to screen us
> each from the other's self : muteness or hesitation,
> nor petrify live miracle by our indifference.

THE ESSENTIAL
MURIEL RUKEYSER

NOTES FOR A POEM

Here are the long fields inviolate of thought,
here are the planted fields raking the sky,
signs in the earth :
water-cast shuttles of light flickering the underside of rock.
These have been shown before; but the fields know new hands,
the son's fingers grasp warmly at the father's hoe ;
there will be new ways of seeing these ancestral lands.

"In town, the munitions plant has been poor since the war,
And nothing but a war will make it rich again."
Holy, holy, holy, sings the church next door.

Time-ridden, a man strides the current of a stream's flowing,
stands, flexing the wand curvingly over his head,
tracking the water's prism with the flung line.
Summer becomes productive and mature.
Farmers watch tools like spikes of doom against the sure
condemning sky descending upon the hollow lands.

The water is ridged in muscles on the rock,
force for the State is planted in the stream-bed.
Water springs from the stone — the State is fed.

Morning comes, brisk with light,
a broom of color over the threshold.
Long flights of shadows escape to the white sky :
a spoon is straightened.   Day grows.   The sky is blued.

The water rushes over the shelves of stone
to anti-climax on the mills below the drop.
The planted fields are bright and rake the sky.
Power is common.   Earth is grown
and overgrown in unrelated strength, the moral
rehearsed already, often.
(There must be the gearing of these facts
into coördination, in a poem or numbers,
rows of statistics, or the cool iambs.)
The locked relationships which will be found
are a design to build these factual timbers —
a plough of thought to break this stubborn ground.

EFFORT AT SPEECH BETWEEN TWO PEOPLE

: Speak to me.   Take my hand.   What are you now?
I will tell you all.   I will conceal nothing.
When I was three, a little child read a story about a rabbit
who died, in the story, and I crawled under a chair :
a pink rabbit : it was my birthday, and a candle
burnt a sore spot on my finger, and I was told to be happy.

: Oh, grow to know me.   I am not happy.   I will be open:
Now I am thinking of white sails against a sky like music,
like glad horns blowing, and birds tilting, and an arm about me.
There was one I loved, who wanted to live, sailing.

: Speak to me.   Take my hand.   What are you now?
When I was nine, I was fruitily sentimental,
fluid : and my widowed aunt played Chopin,
and I bent my head on the painted woodwork, and wept.
I want now to be close to you.   I would
link the minutes of my days close, somehow, to your days.

: I am not happy.   I will be open.
I have liked lamps in evening corners, and quiet poems.
There has been fear in my life.   Sometimes I speculate
On what a tragedy his life was, really.

: Take my hand.   Fist my mind in your hand.   What are you now?
  When I was fourteen, I had dreams of suicide,
  and I stood at a steep window, at sunset, hoping toward death :
  if the light had not melted clouds and plains to beauty,
  if light had not transformed that day, I would have leapt.
  I am unhappy.   I am lonely.   Speak to me.

: I will be open.   I think he never loved me:
  he loved the bright beaches, the little lips of foam
  that ride small waves, he loved the veer of gulls:
  he said with a gay mouth: I love you.   Grow to know me.

: What are you now?   If we could touch one another,
  if these our separate entities could come to grips,
  clenched like a Chinese puzzle . . . yesterday
  I stood in a crowded street that was live with people,
  and no one spoke a word, and the morning shone.
  Everyone silent, moving. . . . Take my hand.   Speak to me.

SONNET

My thoughts through yours refracted into speech
transmute this room musically tonight,
the notes of contact flowing, rhythmic, bright
with an informal art beyond my single reach.

Outside, dark birds fly in a greening time :
wings of our sistered wishes beat these walls :
and words afflict our minds in near footfalls
approaching with a latening hour's chime.

And if an essential thing has flown between us,
rare intellectual bird of communication,
let us seize it quickly : let our preference
choose it instead of softer things to screen us
each from the other's self : muteness or hesitation,
nor petrify live miracle by our indifference.

THIS HOUSE, THIS COUNTRY

Always I travelled farther
dreading a barrier
starting at shadows scattered on the ground
fearful of the invisible night-sound,

till in that straight career
I crossed frontier
the questions asked   the proofs shown   the name
signed smiling   I reached knowledge of my home.

I praised their matings
and corner-meetings
their streets the brightest I had yet walked down :
my family swore I did not leave my town

thought that I lied
and had not signed
those passports, tickets, contracts, bills of sale
but still rested among them and wished them well.

Over my shoulder
I see they grow older

their vision fails : observe I travel light
fear distance   hope I shall only spend the night.

But night in this country
is deep promise of day,
is busy with preparations and awake for fighting
and there is no time for leavetaking and regretting.

I know their tired house
full of remorse
I know in my body the door, the entrance-hall
a wall and my space and another wall.

I have left forever
house and maternal river
given up sitting in that private tomb
quitted that land   that house   that velvet room.

Frontiers admitted me
to a growing country
I carry the proofs of my birth and my mind's reasons
but reckon with their struggle and their seasons.

SAND-QUARRY WITH MOVING FIGURES

Father and I drove to the sand-quarry across the ruined marshlands,
miles of black grass, burned for next summer's green.
I reached my hand to his beneath the lap-robe,
we looked at the stripe of fire, the blasted scene.

"It's all right," he said, "they can control the flames,
on one side men are standing, and on the other the sea;"
but I was terrified of stubble and waste of black
and his ugly villages he built and was showing me.

The countryside turned right and left about the car,
straight through October we drove to the pit's heart;
sand, and its yellow canyon and standing pools
and the wealth of the split country set us farther apart.
"Look," he said, "this quarry means rows of little houses,
stucco and a new bracelet for you are buried there;"
but I remembered the ruined patches, and I saw the land ruined,
exploded, burned away, and the fiery marshes bare.

"We'll own the countryside, you'll see how soon I will,
you'll have acres to play in" : I saw the written name
painted on stone in the face of the steep hill:
"That's your name, Father!"   "And yours!" he shouted, laughing.
"No, Father, no!"   He caught my hand as I cried,
and smiling, entered the pit, ran laughing down its side.

FOR MEMORY

for Ruth Lehman
obit February 10, 1934

Life and Works

Open with care the journal of those years
firm years precipitating days to death
This was my friend walking in color and flame
walking through a texture of sense
                                        no breath
deranges her fine hair   no voice changes her face.

It is hardly possible she will not come again
returned for a short while out of distances
to be re-given to distance and her loves.
It is hardly truth to say that soon
a letter will not come, postmarked Detroit,
New Orleans, Chicago, ultimate Mexico.
I think she must come, and go, and come again.

Throatfuls of life, arms crammed with brilliant days,
the colored years beat strength upon her youth,
pain-bombs exploded her body, joy rocketed in her,

the stranger forests, the books, the bitter times,
preluded college in a sheltered town.
        Remembering the pale suede jacket and russet coat
        swinging down avenues of trees together,
        the nights of talk   light cast from copper bowls,
        the fugitive journey to the coal-hills : names,
        Del Thomas, Tony Mancuso, Mrs. Silva
        the black river curdling under a midnight wind.
        Remembering how the pale wrists flickered love,
        the dark eye-sockets impelled her to the poor,
            ring changes
            tell of the loves in her life
            tell how she loved.
This was my friend of whom I knew the face
the steel-straight intellect, broidered fantastic dreams
the quarrel by the lake
and knew the hopes

        She died.   And must be dead.
And is not dead where memory prevails.

Cut the stone, deepen her name.
Her mother did not know her.
Her friends were not enough, we missed essentials.
Love was enough and its blossoms.   Behind her life
stands a tall flower-tree, around her life

are worked her valid words into her testament
of love and writing and a ring of love.

Holy Dying

Across the country, iron hands push up chimneys
black fingers stuck up from the blackened ground.
The rivers bend seaward urgent in blue reaches;
her pain turned seaward.   Her life extended past
the sea, the cities, the individual poor,
passionate and companioned, following life.

Through the bright years reckless and proud
dimming into that last impossible pain.
We cannot think she will not come again.
The words lean on the written line, the page
is a signal fire   all the letters shine.
Into this life is lowered now death's sign,
the younger days flicker up, the poems burn,
we cannot say Return.

Slowly her death is propelled into our lives
the yellow message   the clipped convenient style
the cancelled stamps   the telephone wires ring
confirming fear "You were right" : in a week's short while.

Her love was never handcuffed, her hates spoke up,
her life was a job of freedom.

                    Now the news comes, the *Times* prints a name
                    the telephone rings short music over her.
Drink your coffee, open your throat for words.
Loving, she died in passion and holiness.
They share remorse who had required less.

Ritual for Death

Last night she died
Turn down the lamps tonight
shade the walls
                let the proud voices rise
out of the midnight street,   the whistle flying
up and along and flying in the street
the harsh struck stone,   a brake squealing the pause
and the brave silence after a lapse of sound.

Turn out the lights
Her body does not move
is striding over no hill in all the world
there is no avenue in Illinois shall know
the eager mouth,   the fine voluptuous hands
touch no more Mexicos in dream again.

There was a shadow deep along her cheek,
her eyes and hair were intricate with sun.
Now lights are out.
:   Stand to me in the dark
Set your mouth on me for friends we did not know

Be strong in love
give strength to all we meet
the loving   the kind   the proletarian strong
convey our love to her in the grey fields
less grey for her, send her our breathing lives.
This was my friend
                              forget the "my," speak out
This was my friend who   eager   rash   and brave
has found one answer in an early grave.
This is my body : in its youth I find
strength given from the startle of her mind.
If we have strength in this evening, force life between her lips
     seal it   convey it   post it   the sheet discolored
     the ink already fading
                              the dead words fading
                              the dead all dead.

Out of the South are vivid flowers sent,
African daisies, red anemone :
here are the riches of a continent,

and intellectual gifts   breaking you free,
poetry sounding in the narrow skull
sealing the sutures with music,   smoothing the cheek
with vocable comfort   the long hands of sorrow.
The full-blown flowers are given : our hands are full
of flowers and gestures : across New England dunes
where the stiff grasses rise against the sea,
across the city   the dark-red roofs, the stone,
across the Alleghanies,   down the Valley
the air speaks plenty   the words have all been spoken.

        Upon what skies are these ambitions written?
        across what field lies scattered the young wish,
        beneath what seas toll all those fallen dreams—?

CITY OF MONUMENTS

Washington 1934

Be proud   you people   of these graves
       these chiseled words   this precedent
From these blind ruins shines our monument.
Dead navies of the brain will sail
       stone celebrate its final choice
       when the air shakes, a single voice
a strong voice able to prevail :

Entrust no hope to stone although the stone
shelter the root : see too-great burdens placed
with nothing certain but the risk
set on the infirm column of
the high memorial obelisk

       erect in accusation sprung against
a barren sky taut over Anacostia :
give over, Gettysburg   !   a word will shake your glory :
blood of the starved fell thin upon this plain,
this battle is not buried with its slain.

Gravestone and battlefield retire
the whole green South is shadowed dark,
the slick white domes are cast in night.
But uneclipsed above the park

the veteran of the Civil War
sees havoc in the tended graves
the midnight bugles blown to free
still unemancipated slaves.

Blinded by chromium or transfiguration
we watch, as through a microscope, decay :
   down the broad streets the limousines
advance in passions of display.

Air glints with diamonds, and these clavicles
emerge through orchids by whose trailing spoor
the sensitive cannot mistake
the implicit anguish of the poor.

The throats incline, the marble men rejoice
careless of torrents of despair.

Split by a tendril of revolt
stone cedes to blossom everywhere.

METAPHOR TO ACTION

Whether it is a speaker, taut on a platform,
who battles a crowd with the hammers of his words,
whether it is the crash of lips on lips
after absence and wanting : we must close
the circuits of ideas, now generate,
that leap in the body's action or the mind's repose.

Over us is a striking on the walls of the sky,
here are the dynamos, steel-black, harboring flame,
here is the man night-walking who derives
tomorrow's manifestoes from this midnight's meeting ;
here we require the proof in solidarity,
iron on iron, body on body, and the large single beating.

And behind us in time are the men who second us
as we continue.   And near us is our love :
no forced contempt, no refusal in dogma, the close
of the circuit in a fierce dazzle of purity.
And over us is night a field of pansies unfolding,
charging with heat its softness in a symbol
to weld and prepare for action our minds' intensity.

THE BLOOD IS JUSTIFIED

Beat out continuance in the choking veins
before emotion betrays us, and we find
staring behind our faces, accomplices of death.
Not to die, but slowly to validate our lives :
simply to move, lightly burdened, alone,
carrying in this brain survival, carrying
within these ribs, history,
the past deep in the bone.

Unthread time till its empty needle prick your flesh
sewing your scars with air, treating the wounds
only by laceration   and the blood is fresh
blood on our skin on our lips over our eyes.

Living they move on a canvas of centuries
restored from death in artful poses, found
once more by us, descendants, foraging,
ravelling time back over American ground.
How did they wish, grandparents of these wars,
what cataracts of ambition fell across their brains? :

The heavy boots kicked stones down Wisconsin roads,
Augusta Coller danced her début at Oshkosh :
they spoke these names : Milwaukee, Waukesha,
the crackle and drawl of Indian strange words.

Jungle-savage the south
raw green and shining branches, the crying
of parakeets, the pointed stone,
the altars stained with oil :
Mexico : and Canada wheaten and polar with
snow halfway up the sky :
all these unknown.

: What treason to their race has fathered us?
They walked in the towns, the men selling clothing etc.
the women tatting and boiling down grape jelly.
: If they were asked this, surely they did not answer.

Over the country, Wisconsin, Chicago, Yonkers,
I was begotten, American branch no less because
I call on the great names of other countries.
I do not say : Forgive, to my kindred dead,
only : Understand my treason, See I betray you kissing,
I overthrow your milestones weeping among your tombs.

From out your knowing eyes I sprang, child of your distant wombs,
of your full lips.   Speaking allegiance, I turn,
steadfastly to destroy your hope   Your cargo in me
swings to ports hostile to your old intent.

In us recurrences. : My generation feeds
the wise assault on your anticipation,
repeating historic sunderings, betraying our fathers,
all parricidal in our destinies.

How much are we American?   Not knowing
those other lands, being
blood wrung from your bone, our pioneers,
we call kindred to you, we claim links, speaking
your tongue, although we pass, shaking
your dream with revolution since we must.
By these roads shall we come upon our country.
Pillowed upon this birthright, we may wake
strong for such treason, brave with your fallen dust.

O, we are afflicted with these present evils,
they press between the mirror and our eyes,
obscuring your loaned mouths and borrowed hair.
We focus on our times, destroying you, fathers
in the long ground : you have given strange birth

to us who turn against you in our blood
needing to move in our integrity, accomplices
of life in revolution, though the past
be sweet with your tall shadows, and although
we turn from treasons, we shall accomplish these.

THE ROAD

These are roads to take when you think of your country
and interested bring down the maps again,
phoning the statistician, asking the dear friend,

reading the papers with morning inquiry.
Or when you sit at the wheel and your small light
chooses gas gauge and clock; and the headlights

indicate future of road, your wish pursuing
past the junction, the fork, the suburban station,
well-travelled six-lane highway planned for safety.

Past your tall central city's influence,
outside its body: traffic, penumbral crowds,
are centers removed and strong, fighting for good reason.

These roads will take you into your own country.
Select the mountains, follow rivers back,
travel the passes. Touch West Virginia where

the Midland Trail leaves the Virginia furnace,
iron Clifton Forge, Covington iron, goes down
into the wealthy valley, resorts, the chalk hotel.

Pillars and fairway; spa; White Sulphur Springs.
Airport. Gay blank rich faces wishing to add
history to ballrooms, tradition to the first tee.

The simple mountains, sheer, dark-graded with pine
in the sudden weather, wet outbreak of spring,
crosscut by snow, wind at the hill's shoulder.

The land is fierce here, steep, braced against snow,
rivers and spring. KING COAL HOTEL, Lookout,
and swinging the vicious bend, New River Gorge.

Now the photographer unpacks camera and case,
surveying the deep country, follows discovery
viewing on groundglass an inverted image.

John Marshall named the rock (steep pines, a drop
he reckoned in 1812, called) Marshall's Pillar,
but later, Hawk's Nest. Here is your road, tying

you to its meanings: gorge, boulder, precipice.
Telescoped down, the hard and stone-green river
cutting fast and direct into the town.

WEST VIRGINIA

They saw rivers flow west and hoped again.
Virginia speeding to another sea!
1671—Thomes Batts, Robert Fallam,
Thomas Wood, the Indian Perecute,
and an unnamed indentured English servant
followed the forest past blazed trees, pillars of God,
were the first whites emergent from the east.
They left a record to our heritage,
breaking of records. Hoped now for the sea,
For all mountaines have their descents about them,
waters, descending naturally, doe alwaies resort
unto the seas invironing those lands . . .
Yea, at home amongst the mountaines in England.

Coming where this road comes,
flat stones spilled water which the still pools fed.
Kanawha Falls, the rapids of the mind,
fast waters spilling west.

Found Indian fields, standing low cornstalks left,
learned three Mohetons planted them; found-land
farmland, the planted home, discovered!

War-born:
The battle at Point Pleasant, Cornstalk's tribes,
last stand, Fort Henry, a revolution won;
the granite SITE OF THE precursor EXECUTION
sabres, apostles OF JOHN BROWN LEADER OF THE
War's brilliant cloudy RAID AT HARPERS FERRY.
Floods, heavy wind this spring, the beaten land
blown high by wind, fought wars, forming a state,
a surf, frontier defines two fighting halves,
two hundred battles in the four years: troops
here in Gauley Bridge, Union headquarters, lines
bring in the military telegraph.
Wires over the gash of gorge and height of pine.

But it was always the water
the power flying deep
green rivers cut the rock
rapids boiled down,
a scene of power.

Done by the dead.
Discovery learned it.
And the living?

Live country filling west,
knotted the glassy rivers;
like valleys, opening mines,
coming to life.

STATEMENT: PHILIPPA ALLEN

—You like the State of West Virginia very much, do you not?

—I do very much, in the summertime.

—How much time have you spent in West Virginia?

—During the summer of 1934, when I was doing social work
　　　down there, I first heard of what we were pleased to call the
　　　Gauley tunnel tragedy, which involved about 2,000 men.

—What was their salary?

—It started at 40¢ and dropped to 25¢ an hour.

—You have met these people personally?

—I have talked to people; yes.

　According to estimates of contractors

　2,000 men were

　　　　employed there

　　　　period, about 2 years

　　　　drilling, 3.75 miles of tunnel.

　　　　To divert water (from New River)

　　　　to a hydroelectric plant (at Gauley Junction).

The rock through which they were boring was of a high
　silica content.

In tunnel No. 1 it ran 97–99% pure silica.

The contractors

　　　　knowing pure silica

30 years' experience
    must have known danger for every man
neglected to provide the workmen with any safety device. . . .
—As a matter of fact, they originally intended to dig that
    tunnel a certain size?
—Yes.
—And then enlarged the size of the tunnel, due to the fact
    that they discovered silica and wanted to get it out?
—That is true for tunnel No. 1.
    The tunnel is part of a huge water-power project
            begun, latter part of 1929
            direction: New Kanawha Power Co.
                    subsidiary of Union Carbide & Carbon Co.
            That company—licensed:
            to develop power for public sale.
            Ostensibly it was to do that; but
            (in reality) it was formed to sell all the power to
                    the Electro-Metallurgical Co.
                    subsidiary of Union Carbide & Carbon Co.
                    which by an act of the State legislature
                    was allowed to buy up
            New Kanawha Power Co. in 1933.
—They were developing the power. What I am trying to get at,
    Miss Allen, is, did they use this silica from the tunnel; did
    they afterward sell it and use it in commerce?

—They used it in the electro-processing of steel.

SiO_2 SiO_2

The richest deposit.

Shipped on the C & O down to Alloy.

It was so pure that

$$SiO_2$$

they used it without refining.

—Where did you stay?

—I stayed at Cedar Grove. Some days I would have to hitch
    into Charleston, other days to Gauley Bridge.

—You found the people of West Virginia very happy to pick
    you up on the highway, did you not?

—Yes; they are delightfully obliging.

(All were bewildered. Again at Vanetta they are asking,
    "What can be done about this?")

I feel that this investigation may help in some manner.

I do hope it may.

I am now making a very general statement as a beginning.

There are many points that I should like to develop later,
    but I shall try to give you a general history of this
    condition first. . . .

GAULEY BRIDGE

Camera at the crossing sees the city
a street of wooden walls and empty windows,
the doors shut handless in the empty street,
and the deserted Negro standing on the corner.

The little boy runs with his dog
up the street to the bridge over the river where
nine men are mending road for the government.
He blurs the camera-glass fixed on the street.

Railway tracks here and many panes of glass
tin under light, the grey shine of towns and forests:
in the commercial hotel (Switzerland of America)
the owner is keeping his books behind the public glass.

Post office window, a hive of private boxes,
the hand of the man who withdraws, the woman who reaches
    her hand
and the tall coughing man stamping an envelope.

The bus station and the great pale buses stopping for food;
April-glass-tinted, the yellow-aproned waitress;
coast-to-coast schedule on the plateglass window.

The man on the street and the camera eye:
he leaves the doctor's office, slammed door, doom,
any town looks like this one-street town.

Glass, wood, and naked eye : the movie-house
closed for the afternoon frames posters streaked with rain,
advertise "Racing Luck" and "Hitch-Hike Lady."

Whistling, the train comes from a long way away,
slow, and the Negro watches it grow in the grey air,
the hotel man makes a note behind his potted palm.

Eyes of the tourist house, red-and-white filling station,
the eyes of the Negro, looking down the track,
hotel-man and hotel, cafeteria, camera.

And in the beerplace on the other sidewalk
always one's harsh night eyes over the beerglass
follow the waitress and the yellow apron.

The road flows over the bridge,
Gamoca pointer at the underpass,
opposite, Alloy, after a block of town.

What do you want—a cliff over a city?
A foreland, sloped to sea and overgrown with roses?
These people live here.

THE FACE OF THE DAM:
VIVIAN JONES

On the hour he shuts the door and walks out of town;
he knows the place up the gorge where he can see
his locomotive rusted on the siding,
he sits and sees the river at his knee.

There, where the men crawl, landscaping the grounds
at the power-plant, he saw the blasts explode
the mouth of the tunnel that opened wider
when precious in the rock the white glass showed.

The old plantation-house (burned to the mud)
is a hill-acre of ground. The Negro woman throws
gay arches of water out from the front door.
It runs down, wild as grass, falls and flows.

On the quarter he remembers how they enlarged
the tunnel and the crews, finding the silica,
how the men came riding freights, got jobs here
and went into the tunnel-mouth to stay.

Never to be used, he thinks, never to spread its power,
jinx on the rock, curse on the power-plant,

hundreds breathed value, filled their lungs full of glass
(O the gay wind the clouds the many men).

On the half-hour he's at Hawk's Nest over the dam,
snow springs up as he reaches the great wall-face,
immense and pouring power, the mist of snow,
the fallen mist, the slope of water, glass.

O the gay snow the white dropped water, down,
all day the water rushes down its river,
unused, has done its death-work in the country,
proud gorge and festive water.

On the last quarter he pulls his heavy collar up,
feels in his pocket the picture of his girl,
touches for luck—he used to as he drove
after he left his engine; stamps in the deep snow.

And the snow clears and the dam stands in the gay weather,
O proud O white O water rolling down,
he turns and stamps this off his mind again
and on the hour walks again through town.

PRAISE OF THE COMMITTEE

These are the lines on which a committee is formed.
   Almost as soon as work was begun in the tunnel
   men began to die among dry drills. No masks.
   Most of them were not from this valley.
   The freights brought many every day from States
   all up and down the Atlantic seaboard
   and as far inland as Kentucky, Ohio.
   After the work the camps were closed or burned.
   The ambulance was going day and night,
   White's undertaking business thriving and
   his mother's cornfield put to a new use.
   "Many of the shareholders at this meeting
   were nervous about the division of the profits;
   How much has the Company spent on lawsuits?
   The man said $150,000. Special counsel:
   I am familiar with the case. Not : one : cent.
   'Terms of the contract. Master liable.'
   No reply. Great corporation disowning men who made. . . ."
   After the lawsuits had been instituted. . . .
The Committee is a true reflection of the will of the people.
   Every man is ill. The women are not affected,

This is not a contagious disease. A medical commission,
Dr. Hughes, Dr. Hayhurst examined the chest
of Raymond Johnson, and Dr. Harless, a former
company doctor. But he saw too many die,
he has written his letter to Washington.
The Committee meets regularly, wherever it can.
Here are Mrs. Jones, three lost sons, husband sick,
Mrs. Leek, cook for the bus cafeteria,
the men : George Robinson, leader and voice,
four other Negroes (three drills, one camp-boy)
Blankenship, the thin friendly man, Peyton the engineer,
Juanita absent, the one outsider member.
Here in the noise, loud belts of the shoe-repair shop,
meeting around the stove beneath the one bulb hanging.
They come late in the day. Many come with them
who pack the hall, wait in the thorough dark.
This is a defense committee. Unfinished business:
Two rounds of lawsuits, 200 cases
Now as to the crooked lawyers
If the men had worn masks, their use would have involved
time every hour to wash the sponge at mouth.
Tunnel, 3 1/8 miles long. Much larger than
the Holland Tunnel or Pittsburgh's Liberty Tubes.
Total cost, say, $16,000,000.

This is the procedure of such a committee:
  To consider the bill before the Senate.
  To discuss relief.
    Active members may be cut off relief,
      16-mile walk to Fayetteville for cheque—
      WEST VIRGINIA RELIEF ADMINISTRATION, #22991,
      TO JOE HENIGAN, GAULEY BRIDGE, ONE AND 50/100,
      WINONA NATIONAL BANK. PAID FROM STATE FUNDS.
  Unless the Defense Committee acts;
  the *People's Press*, supporting this fight,
  signed editorials, sent in funds.
  Clothing for tunnel-workers.
    Rumored, that in the post office
    parcels are intercepted.
    Suspected : Conley. Sheriff, hotelman,
    head of the town ring—
    Company whispers. Spies,
    The Racket.
  Resolved, resolved.
  George Robinson holds all their strength together:
  To fight the companies   to make somehow a future.

"At any rate, it is inadvisable to keep a community of dying
persons intact."

"Senator Holt. Yes. This is the most barbarous example of
industrial construction that ever happened in the world."
Please proceed.
"In a very general way Hippocrates' *Epidemics* speaks
     of the metal digger who breathes with difficulty,
     having a pain and wan complexion.
     Pliny, the elder. . . ."
"Present work of the Bureau of Mines. . . ."

The dam's pure crystal slants upon the river.
     A dark and noisy room, frozen two feet from stove.
     The cough of habit. The sound of men in the hall
     waiting for word.

          These men breathe hard
          but the committee has a voice of steel.
          One climbs the hill on canes.
          They have broken the hills and cracked the riches wide.

          In this man's face
          family leans out from two worlds of graves—
          here is a room of eyes,
          a single force looks out, reading our life.

          Who stands over the river?
          Whose feet go running in these rigid hills?

Who comes, warning the night,
shouting and young to waken our eyes?

Who runs through electric wires?
Who speaks down every road?
Their hands touched mastery; now they
demand an answer.

MEARL BLANKENSHIP

He stood against the stove
facing the fire—
Little warmth, no words,
loud machines.

Voted relief,
wished money mailed,
quietly under the crashing:

"I wake up choking, and my wife
rolls me over on my left side;
then I'm asleep in the dream I always see:
the tunnel choked
the dark wall coughing dust.

I have written a letter.
Send it to the city,
maybe to a paper
if it's all right."

Dear Sir, my name is Mearl Blankenship.
I have Worked for the rhinehart & Dennis Co
Many days & many nights

& it was so dusty you couldn't hardly see the lights.
I helped nip steel for the drills
& helped lay the track in the tunnel
& done lots of drilling near the mouth of the tunnell
& when the shots went off the boss said
If you are going to work Venture back
& the boss was Mr. Andrews
& now he is dead and gone
But I am still here
a lingering along

He stood against the rock
facing the river
grey river grey face
the rock mottled behind him
like X-ray plate enlarged
diffuse and stony
his face against the stone.

J C Dunbar said that I was the very picture of health
when I went to Work at that tunnel.
I have lost eighteen lbs on that Rheinhart ground
and expecting to loose my life
& no settlement yet & I have sued the Co. twice
But when the lawyers got a settlement
they didn't want to talk to me

But I didn't know whether they were sleepy or not.
I am a Married Man and have a family.   God
knows if they can do anything for me
it will be appreciated
if you can do anything for me
let me know soon

ABSALOM

I first discovered what was killing these men.
I had three sons who worked with their father in the tunnel:
Cecil, aged 23, Owen, aged 21, Shirley, aged 17.
They used to work in a coal mine, not steady work
for the mines were not going much of the time.
A power Co. foreman learned that we made home brew,
he formed a habit of dropping in evenings to drink,
persuading the boys and my husband—
give up their jobs and take this other work.
It would pay them better.
Shirley was my youngest son; the boy.
He went into the tunnel.

> *My heart   my mother   my heart   my mother*
> *My heart   my coming into being.*

My husband is not able to work.
He has it, according to the doctor.
We have been having a very hard time making a living since
       this trouble came to us.
I saw the dust in the bottom of the tub.
The boy worked there about eighteen months,
came home one evening with a shortness of breath.

He said, "Mother, I cannot get my breath."
Shirley was sick about three months.
I would carry him from his bed to the table,
from his bed to the porch, in my arms.

> *My heart is mine in the place of hearts,*
> *They gave me back my heart, it lies in me.*

When they took sick, right at the start, I saw a doctor.
I tried to get Dr. Harless to X-ray the boys.
He was the only man I had any confidence in,
the company doctor in the Kopper's mine,
but he would not see Shirley.
He did not know where his money was coming from.
I promised him half if he'd work to get compensation,
but even then he would not do anything.
I went on the road and begged the X-ray money,
the Charleston hospital made the lung pictures,
he took the case after the pictures were made.
And two or three doctors said the same thing.
The youngest boy did not get to go down there with me,
he lay and said, "Mother, when I die,
I want you to have them open me up and
see if that dust killed me.
Try to get compensation,
you will not have any way of making your living

when we are gone,
and the rest are going too."

> *I have gained mastery over my heart*
> *I have gained mastery over my two hands*
> *I have gained mastery over the waters*
> *I have gained mastery over the river.*

The case of my son was the first of the line of lawsuits.
They sent the lawyers down and the doctors down;
they closed the electric sockets in the camps.
There was Shirley, and Cecil, Jeffrey and Oren,
Raymond Johnson, Clev and Oscar Anders,
Frank Lynch, Henry Palf, Mr. Pitch, a foreman;
a slim fellow who carried steel with my boys,
his name was Darnell, I believe. There were many others,
the towns of Glen Ferris, Alloy, where the white rock lies,
six miles away; Vanetta, Gauley Bridge,
Gamoca, Lockwood, the gullies,
the whole valley is witness.
I hitchlike eighteen miles, they make checks out.
They asked me how I keep the cow on $2.
I said one week, feed for the cow, one week, the children's
    flour.
The oldest son was twenty-three.
The next son was twenty-one.

The youngest son was eighteen.
They called it pneumonia at first.
They would pronounce it fever.
Shirley asked that we try to find out.
That's how they learned what the trouble was.

I open out a way, they have covered my sky with crystal
I come forth by day, I am born a second time,
I force a way through, and I know the gate
I shall journey over the earth among the living.

He shall not be diminished, never;
I shall give a mouth to my son.

THE DISEASE

This is a lung disease. Silicate dust makes it.
The dust causing the growth of

This is the X-ray picture taken last April.
I would point out to you : these are the ribs;
this is the region of the breastbone;
this is the heart (a wide white shadow filled with blood).
In here of course is the swallowing tube, esophagus.
The windpipe. Spaces between the lungs.

Between the ribs?

Between the ribs. These are the collar bones.
Now, this lung's mottled, beginning, in these areas.
You'd say a snowstorm had struck the fellow's lungs.
About alike, that side and this side, top and bottom.
The first stage in this period in this case.

Let us have the second.

Come to the window again. Here is the heart.
More numerous nodules, thicker, see, in the upper lobes.

You will notice the increase : here, streaked fibrous tissue—

Indicating?

That indicates the progress in ten months' time.
And now, this year—short breathing, solid scars
even over the ribs, thick on both sides.
Blood vessels shut. Model conglomeration.

What stage?

Third stage. Each time I place my pencil point:
There and there and there, there, there.

    "It is growing worse every day. At night
    I get up to catch my breath. If I remained
    flat on my back I believe I would die."

    It gradually chokes off the air cells in the lungs?
    I am trying to say it the best I can.
    That is what happens, isn't it?
    A choking-off in the air cells?

Yes.
    There is difficulty in breathing.

Yes.

And a painful cough?

Yes.

Does silicosis cause death?

Yes, sir.

GEORGE ROBINSON: BLUES

Gauley Bridge is a good town for Negroes, they let us stand
      around, they let us stand
around on the sidewalks if we're black or brown.
Vanetta's over the trestle, and that's our town.

The hill makes breathing slow, slow breathing after you
      row the river,
and the graveyard's on the hill, cold in the springtime blow,
the graveyard's up on high, and the town is down below.

Did you ever bury thirty-five men in a place in back of your
      house,
thirty-five tunnel workers the doctors didn't attend,
died in the tunnel camps, under rocks, everywhere, world
      without end.

When a man said I feel poorly, for any reason, any weakness
      or such,
letting up when he couldn't keep going barely,
the Cap and company come and run him off the job surely.

I've put them
DOWN from the tunnel camps

to the graveyard on the hill,
tin-cans all about—it fixed them!—

TUNNELITIS
hold themselves up
at the side of a tree,
I can go right now
to that cemetery.

When the blast went off the boss would call out, Come, let's
        go back,
when that heavy loaded blast went white, Come, let's go back,
telling us hurry, hurry, into the falling rocks and muck.

The water they would bring had dust in it, our drinking
        water,
the camps and their groves were colored with the dust,
we cleaned our clothes in the groves, but we always had
        the dust.

Looked like somebody sprinkled flour all over the parks
        and groves,
it stayed and the rain couldn't wash it away and it twinkled
that white dust really looked pretty down around our ankles.

As dark as I am, when I came out at morning after the
    tunnel at night,
with a white man, nobody could have told which man was
    white.
The dust had covered us both, and the dust was white.

JUANITA TINSLEY

Even after the letters, there is work,
sweaters, the food, the shoes
and afternoon's quick dark

draws on the windowpane
my face, the shadowed hair,
the scattered papers fade.

Slow letters! I shall be
always—the stranger said
"To live stronger and free."

I know in America there are songs,
forgetful ballads to be sung,
but at home I see this wrong.

When I see my family house,
the gay gorge, the picture-books,
they raise the face of General Wise

aged by enemies, like faces
the stranger showed me in the town.
I saw that plain, and saw my place.

The scene of hope's ahead; look, April,
and next month with a softer wind,
maybe they'll rest upon their land,
and then maybe the happy song, and love,
a tall boy who was never in a tunnel.

THE DOCTORS

—Tell the jury your name.
—Emory R. Hayhurst.
—State your education, Doctor, if you will.
  Don't be modest about it; just tell about it.

High school Chicago 1899
Univ. of Illinois 1903
M.A. 1905, thesis on respiration
P & S Chicago 1908
2 years' hospital training;
at Rush on occupational disease
director of clinic 2½ years.
Ph.D. Chicago 1916
Ohio Dept. of Health, 20 years as
consultant in occupational diseases.
Hygienist, U.S. Public Health Service
and Bureau of Mines
and Bureau of Standards

Danger begins at 25%
here was pure danger
Dept. of Mines
came in, was kept away.

Miner's phthisis, fibroid phthisis,
grinder's rot, potter's rot,
whatever it used to be called,
these men did not need to die.

—Is silicosis an occupational disease?
—It is.
—Did anyone show you the lungs of Cecil Jones?
—Yes, sir.
—Who was that?
—It was Dr. Harless.

"We talked to Dr. L. R. Harless, who had handled many of the cases, more than any other doctor there. At first Dr. Harless did not like to talk about the matter. He said he had been subjected to so much publicity. It appeared that the doctor thought he had been involved in too many of the court cases; but finally he opened up and told us about the matter."

—Did he impress you as one who thought this was a very serious thing in that section of the country?

"Yes, he did. I would say that Dr. Harless has probably become very self-conscious about this matter. I cannot say that he has retracted what he told me, but possibly he had been thrust into the limelight so much that he is more conservative now than when the matter was simply something of local interest."

Dear Sir: Due to illness of my wife and urgent professional duties, I am unable to appear as per your telegram.

>Situation exaggerated. Here are facts:
>
>We examined. 13 dead. 139 had some lung damage.
>
>2 have died since, making 15 deaths.
>
>Press says 476 dead, 2,000 affected and doomed.
>
>I am at a loss to know where those figures were obtained.
>
>At this time, only a few cases here,
>
>and these only moderately affected.
>
>Last death occurred November, 1934.

It has been said that none of the men knew of the hazard connected with the work. This is not correct. Shortly after the work began many of these workers came to me complaining of chest conditions and I warned many of them of the dust hazard and advised them that continued work under these conditions would result in serious lung disease. Disregarding this warning many of the men continued at this work and later brought suit against their employer for damages.

While I am sure that many of these suits were based on meritorious grounds, I am also convinced that many others took advantage of this situation and made out of it nothing less than a racket.

In this letter I have endeavored to give you the facts which came under my observation. . . .

If I can supply further information. . . .

Mr. Marcantonio. A man may be examined a year after he has worked in a tunnel and not show a sign of silicosis, and yet the silicosis may develop later; is not that true?

—Yes, it may develop as many as ten years after.

Mr. Marcantonio. Even basing the statement on the figures, the doctor's claim that this is a racket is not justified?

—No; it would not seem to be justified.

Mr. Marcantonio. I should like to point out that Dr. Harless contradicts his "exaggeration" when he volunteers the following: "I warned many. . . ."

(Mr. Peyton. I do not know. Nobody knew the danger around there.)

Dr. Goldwater. First are the factors involving the individual.

      Under the heading B, external causes.

      Some of the factors which I have in mind—

      those are the facts upon the blackboard,

      the influencing and controlling factors.

Mr. Marcantonio. Those factors would bring about acute silicosis?

Dr. Goldwater. I hope you are not provoked when I say "might."

      Medicine has no hundred percent.

      We speak of possibilities, have opinions.

Mr. Griswold. Doctors testify answering "yes" and "no."

      Don't they?

Dr. Goldwater. Not by the choice of the doctor.

Mr. Griswold. But that is usual, isn't it?

Dr. Goldwater. They do not like to do that.

      A man with a scientific point of view—

        unfortunately there are doctors without that—
        I do not mean to say all doctors are angels—
        but most doctors avoid dogmatic statements.
        avoid assiduously "always," "never."
Mr. Griswold. Best doctor I ever knew said "no" and "yes."
Dr. Goldwater. There are different opinions on that, too.
        We were talking about acute silicosis.

        The man in the white coat is the man on the hill,
        the man with the clean hands is the man with the drill,
        the man who answers "yes" lies still.

    —Did you make an examination of those sets of lungs?
    —I did.
    —I wish you would tell the jury whether or not those lungs
    were silicotic.
    —We object.
    —Objection overruled.
    —They were.

THE CORNFIELD

Error, disease, snow, sudden weather.
For those given to contemplation : this house,
wading in snow, its cracks are sealed with clay,
walls papered with print, newsprint repeating,
in-focus grey across the room, and squared
ads for a book : HEAVEN'S MY DESTINATION,
HEAVEN'S MY . . . HEAVEN . . . . THORNTON WILDER.
The long-faced man rises long-handed jams the door
tight against snow, long-boned, he shivers.
Contemplate.

                    Swear by the corn,
the found-land corn, those who like ritual. *He*
rides in a good car. They say blind corpses rode
with him in front, knees broken into angles,
head clamped ahead. Overalls. Affidavits.
He signs all papers. His office : where he sits.
feet on the stove, loaded trestles through door,
satin-lined, silk-lined, unlined, cheap,
The papers in the drawer. On the desk, photograph
H. C. White, Funeral Services (new car and eldest son);
tells about Negroes who got wet at work,
shot craps, drank and took cold, pneumonia, died.

Shows the sworn papers. Swear by the corn.
Pneumonia, pneumonia, pleurisy, t.b.

For those given to voyages : these roads
discover gullies, invade, Where does it go now?
Now turn upstream twenty-five yards. Now road again.
Ask the man on the road. Saying, That cornfield?
Over the second hill, through the gate,
watch for the dogs. Buried, five at a time,
pine boxes, Rinehart & Dennis paid him $55
a head for burying these men in plain pine boxes.
His mother is suing him: misuse of land.
George Robinson : I knew a man
who died at four in the morning at the camp.
At seven his wife took clothes to dress her dead
husband, and at the undertaker's
they told her the husband was already buried.
—Tell me this, the men with whom you are acquainted,
the men who have this disease
have been told that sooner or later they are going to die?
—Yes, sir.
—How does that seem to affect the majority of the people?
—It don't work on anything but their wind.
—Do they seem to be living in fear
or do they wish to die?
—They are getting to breathe a little faster.

For those given to keeping their own garden:
Here is the cornfield, white and wired by thorns,
old cornstalks, snow, the planted home.
Stands bare against a line of farther field,
unmarked except for wood stakes, charred at tip,
few scratched and named (pencil or nail).
Washed-off. Under the mounds,
all the anonymous.
Abel America, calling from under the corn,
Earth, uncover my blood!
Did the undertaker know the man was married?
Uncover.
Do they seem to fear death?
Contemplate.
Does Mellon's ghost walk, povertied at last,
walking in furrows of corn, still sowing,
do apparitions come?
Voyage.
Think of your gardens. But here is corn to keep.
Marked pointed sticks to name the crop beneath.
Sowing is over, harvest is coming ripe.

—No, sir; they want to go on.
They want to live as long as they can.

ARTHUR PEYTON

Consumed. Eaten away. And love across the street.
I had a letter in the mail this morning
Dear Sir, . . . pleasure . . . enclosing herewith our check . . .
payable to you, for $21.59
       being one-half of the residue which
       we were able to collect in your behalf
       in regard to the above case.
In winding up the various suits,
       after collecting all we could,
       we find this balance due you.
With regards, we are
       Very truly,

After collecting
       the dust   the failure   the engineering corps
O love   consumed   eaten away   the foreman laughed
they wet the drills when the inspectors came
the moon blows glassy over our native river.

O love tell the committee that I know:
never repeat you mean to marry me.
In mines, the fans are large (2,000 men unmasked)
before his verdict the doctor asked me   How long

I said, Dr. Harless, tell me how long?
—Only never again tell me you'll marry me.
I watch how at the tables you all day
follow a line of clouds   the dance of drills,

and, love, the sky birds who crown the trees
the white white hills standing upon Alloy
—I charge negligence, all companies concerned—
two years O love two years he said he gave.

The swirl of river at the tidy house
the marble bank-face of the liquor store
I saw the Negroes driven with pick handles
on these other jobs I was not in tunnel work.

Between us, love

                        the buses at the door
the long glass street   two years, my death to yours
my death upon your lips
my face becoming glass
strong challenged time making me win immortal
the love a mirror of our valley
our street   our river   a deadly glass to hold.
Now they are feeding me into a steel mill furnace
O love the stream of glass a stream of living fire.

ALLOY

This is the most audacious landscape. The gangster's
stance with his gun smoking and out is not so
vicious as this commercial field, its hill of glass.

Sloping as gracefully as thighs, the foothills
narrow to this, clouds over every town
finally indicate the stored destruction.

Crystalline hill: a blinded field of white
murdering snow, seamed by convergent tracks;
the travelling cranes reach for the silica.

And down the track, the overhead conveyor
slides on its cable to the feet of chimneys.
Smoke rises, not white enough, not so barbaric.

Here the severe flame speaks from the brick throat,
electric furnaces produce this precious, this clean,
annealing the crystals, fusing at last alloys.

Hottest for silicon, blast furnaces raise flames,
spill fire, spill steel, quench the new shape to freeze,
tempering it to perfected metal.

Forced through this crucible, a million men.
Above this pasture, the highway passes those
who curse the air, breathing their fear again.

The roaring flowers of the chimney-stacks
less poison, at their lips in fire, than this
dust that is blown from off the field of glass;

blows and will blow, rising over the mills,
crystallized and beyond the fierce corrosion
disintegrated angel on these hills.

THE DISEASE: AFTER-EFFECTS

This is the life of a Congressman.
Now he is standing on the floor of the House,
the galleries full; raises his voice; presents the bill.
Legislative, the fanfare, greeting its heroes with
ringing of telephone bells preceding entrances,
snapshots (Grenz rays, recording structure) newsreels.
This is silent, and he proposes:

                             embargo on munitions

to Germany and Italy
as states at war with Spain.
He proposes

                Congress memorialize
the governor of California : free Tom Mooney.
A bill for a TVA at Fort Peck Dam.
A bill to prevent industrial silicosis.

This is the gentleman from Montana.
—I'm a child, I'm leaning from a bedroom window,
clipping the rose that climbs upon the wall,
the tea roses, and the red roses,
one for a wound, another for disease,
remembrance for strikers. I was five, going on six,
my father on strike at the Anaconda mine;

they broke the Socialist mayor we had in Butte,
the sheriff (friendly), found their judge. Strike-broke.
Shot father. He died : wounds and his disease.
My father had silicosis.

Copper contains it, we find it in limestone,
sand quarries, sandstone, potteries, foundries,
granite, abrasives, blasting; many kinds of grinding,
plate, mining, and glass.

Widespread in trade, widespread in space!
Butte, Montana; Joplin, Missouri; the New York tunnels,
the Catskill Aqueduct. In over thirty States.
A disease worse than consumption.

Only eleven States have laws.
There are today one million potential victims.
500,000 Americans have silicosis now.
These are the proportions of a war.

       Pictures rise, foreign parades, the living faces,
       Asturian miners with my father's face,
       wounded and fighting, the men at Gauley Bridge,
       my father's face enlarged; since now our house

       and all our meaning lies in this
       signature: power on a hill

centered in its committee and its armies
sources of anger, the mine of emphasis.

No plane can ever lift us high enough
to see forgetful countries underneath,
but always now the map and X-ray seem
resemblent pictures of one living breath
one country marked by error
and one air.

It sets up a gradual scar formation;
this increases, blocking all drainage from the lung,
eventually scars, blocking the blood supply,
and then they block the air passageways.
Shortness of breath,
pains around the chest,
he notices lack of vigor.

Bill blocked; investigation blocked.

These galleries produce their generations.
The Congressmen are restless, stare at the triple tier,
the flags, the ranks, the walnut foliage wall;
a row of empty seats, mask over a dead voice.
But over the country, a million look from work,
five hundred thousand stand.

THE BILL

The subcommittee submits:
Your committee held hearings, heard many witnesses; finds:

THAT the Hawk's Nest tunnel was constructed
        Dennis and Rinehart, Charlottesville, Va., for
        New Kanawha Power Co., subsidiary of
        Union Carbide & Carbon Co.

THAT a tunnel was drilled
        app. dist. 3.75 mis.
        to divert water (from New River)
        to hydroelectric plant (Gauley Junction).

THAT in most of the tunnel, drilled rock contained
        90—even 99 percent pure silica.

This is a fact that was known.

THAT silica is dangerous to lungs of human beings.
        When submitted to contact. Silicosis.

THAT the effects are well known.
        Disease incurable.
        Physical incapacity, cases fatal.

THAT the Bureau of Mines has warned for twenty years.

THAT prevention is: wet drilling, ventilation,
                        respirators, vacuum drills.

    Disregard : utter. Dust : collected. Visibility : low.

    Workmen left work, white with dust.

    Air system : inadequate.

    It was quite cloudy in there.

    When the drills were going, in all the smoke and dust,

    it seemed like a gang of airplanes going through

        that tunnel.

    Respirators, not furnished.

    I have seen men with masks, but simply on their breasts.

    I have seen two wear them.

    Drills : dry drilling, for speed, for saving.

    A fellow could drill three holes dry for one hole wet.

    They went so fast they didn't square at the top.

    Locomotives : gasoline. Suffering from monoxide gas.

    There have been men that fell in the tunnel. They had

        to be carried out.

The driving of the tunnel.

    It was begun, continued, completed, with gravest disregard.

    And the employees? Their health, lives, future?

Results and infection.

    Many died. Many are not yet dead.

    Of negligence. Wilful or inexcusable.

Further findings:

       Prevalence : many States, mine, tunnel operations.

       A greatest menace.

We suggest hearings be read.

       This is the dark. Lights strung up all the way.

       Depression; and, driven deeper in,

       by hunger, pistols, and despair,

       they took the tunnel.

Of the contracting firm

             P. H. Faulconer, Pres.

             E. J. Perkins, Vice-Pres.

       have declined to appear.

       They have no knowledge of deaths from silicosis.

       However, their firm paid claims.

       I want to point out that under the statute $500 or

          $1000, but no more, may be recovered.

We recommend.

       Bring them. Their books and records.

       Investigate. Require.

Can do no more.

       These citizens from many States

       paying the price for electric power,

       To Be Vindicated.

"If by their suffering and death they will have made a future life safer for work beneath the earth, if they will have been able to establish a new and greater regard for human life in industry, their suffering may not have been in vain."

Respectfully,
Glenn Griswold
Chairman, Subcommittee
Vito Marcantonio
W.P. Lambertson
Matthew A. Dunn

The subcommittee subcommits.

Words on a monument.
Capitoline thunder. It cannot be enough.
The origin of storms is not in clouds,
our lightning strikes when the earth rises,
spillways free authentic power:
dead John Brown's body walking from a tunnel
to break the armored and concluded mind.

THE BOOK OF THE DEAD

These roads will take you into your own country.
Seasons and maps coming where this road comes
into a landscape mirrored in these men.

Past all your influences, your home river,
constellations of cities, mottoes of childhood,
parents and easy cures, war, all evasion's wishes.

What one word must never be said?
Dead, and these men fight off our dying,
cough in the theatres of the war.

What two things shall never be seen?
They: what we did.   Enemy : what we mean.
This is a nation's scene and halfway house.

What three things can never be done?
Forget.   Keep silent.   Stand alone.
The hills of glass, the fatal brilliant plain.

The facts of war forced into actual grace.
Seasons and modern glory.   Told in the histories,
                how first ships came

seeing on the Atlantic thirteen clouds
lining the west horizon with their white
            shining halations;

they conquered, throwing off impossible Europe—
could not be used to transform; created coast—
            breathed-in America.

See how they took the land, made after-life
fresh out of exile, planted the pioneer
            base and blockade,

pushed forests down in an implacable walk
west where new clouds lay at the desirable
            body of sunset;

taking the seaboard.   Replaced the isolation,
dropped cities where they stood, drew a tidewater
            frontier of Europe,

a moment, and another frontier held,
this land was planted home-land that we know.
            Ridge of discovery,

until we walk to windows, seeing America
lie in a photograph of power, widened
before our forehead,

and still behind us falls another glory,
London unshaken, the long French road to Spain,
the old Mediterranean

flashing new signals from the hero hills
near Barcelona, monuments and powers,
parent defenses.

Before our face the broad and concrete west,
green ripened field, frontier pushed back like river
controlled and dammed;

the flashing wheatfields, cities, lunar plains
grey in Nevada, the sane fantastic country
sharp in the south,

liveoak, the hanging moss, a world of desert,
the dead, the lava, and the extreme arisen
fountains of life,

the flourished land, peopled with watercourses
to California and the colored sea;
sums of frontiers

and unmade boundaries of acts and poems,
the brilliant scene between the seas, and standing,
  this fact and this disease.

  ❧

Half-memories absorb us, and our ritual world
carries its history in familiar eyes,
planted in flesh it signifies its music

in minds which turn to sleep and memory,
in music knowing all the shimmering names,
the spear, the castle, and the rose.

But planted in our flesh these valleys stand,
everywhere we begin to know the illness,
are forced up, and our times confirm us all.

In the museum life, centuries of ambition
yielded at last a fertilizing image:
the Carthaginian stone meaning a tall woman

carries in her two hands the book and cradled dove,
on her two thighs, wings folded from the waist
cross to her feet, a pointed human crown.

This valley is given to us like a glory.
To friends in the old world, and their lifting hands
that call for intercession.   Blow falling full in face.

All those whose childhood made learn skill to meet,
and art to see after the change of heart;
all the belligerents who know the world.

You standing over gorges, surveyors and planners,
you workers and hope of countries, first among powers;
you who give peace and bodily repose,

opening landscapes by grace, giving the marvel lowlands
physical peace, flooding old battlefields
with general brilliance, who best love your lives;

and you young, you who finishing the poem
wish new perfection and begin to make;
you men of fact, measure our times again.

&

These are our strength, who strike against history.
These whose corrupt cells owe their new styles of weakness
                to our diseases;

these carrying light for safety on their foreheads
descended deeper for richer faults of ore,
                drilling their death.

These touching radium and the luminous poison,
carried their death on their lips and with their warning
                glow in their graves.

These weave and their eyes water and rust away,
these stand at wheels until their brains corrode,
these farm and starve,

all these men cry their doom across the world,
meeting avoidable death, fight against madness,
find every war.

Are known as strikers, soldiers, pioneers,
fight on all new frontiers, are set in solid
lines of defense.

Defense is sight; widen the lens and see
standing over the land myths of identity,
new signals, processes:

Alloys begin: certain dominant metals.
Deliberate combines add new qualities,
sums of new uses.

Over the country, from islands of Maine fading,
Cape Sable fading south into the orange
detail of sunset,

new processes, new signals, new possession.
A name for all the conquests, prediction of victory
deep in these powers.

Carry abroad the urgent need, the scene,
to photograph and to extend the voice,
            to speak this meaning.

Voices to speak to us directly.   As we move.
As we enrich, growing in larger motion,
            this word, this power.

Down coasts of taken countries, mastery,
discovery at one hand, and at the other
            frontiers and forests,

fanatic cruel legend at our back and
speeding ahead the red and open west,
            and this our region,

desire, field, beginning.   Name and road,
communication to these many men,
as epilogue, seeds of unending love.

READING TIME : 1 MINUTE 26 SECONDS

The fear of poetry is the
fear : mystery and fury of a midnight street
of windows whose low voluptuous voice
issues, and after that there is no peace.

That round waiting moment in the
theatre : curtain rises, dies into the ceiling
and here is played the scene with the mother
bandaging a revealed son's head. The bandage is torn off.
Curtain goes down. And here is the moment of proof.

That climax when the brain acknowledges the world,
all values extended into the blood awake.
Moment of proof. And as they say Brancusi did,
building his bird to extend through soaring air,
as Kafka planned stories that draw to eternity
through time extended. And the climax strikes.

Love touches so, that months after the look of
blue stare of love, the footbeat on the heart
is translated into the pure cry of birds
following air-cries, or poems, the new scene.
Moment of proof. That strikes long after act.

They fear it. They turn away, hand up palm out
fending off moment of proof, the straight look, poem.
The prolonged wound-consciousness after the bullet's shot.
The prolonged love after the look is dead,
the yellow joy after the song of the sun.

SONG

The world is full of loss; bring, wind, my love,
      My home is where we make our meeting-place,
      And love whatever I shall touch and read
      Within that face.

Lift, wind, my exile from my eyes;
      Peace to look, life to listen and confess,
      Freedom to find to find to find
      That nakedness.

LOVE AND ITS DOORS AND WINDOWS

History melts my houses,
But they were all one house
Where in the dark beginning
A tall and maniac nurse
Hid tortures behind the door
And afterwards kissed me
Promising all as before.

The second house was music;
The childish hands of fear
Lying on a piano
That was blackness and light,
Opened my life with sound—
Extorting promises
Loud in the ringing air.

After that, broken houses,
The wealthy halls of cloud
Haunted by living parents
And the possessive face.
Power and outrage looking
At the great river
Marvellous filthy and gold.

When love lay in my arms
I all night kissed that mouth,
And the incredible body
Slept warm at my side;
But the walls fell apart
Among my lifetime dream—
O, a voice said crying,
My mother's broken heart.

Nothing was true in the sense
I wanted it to be true.
Victory came late,
Excitement returned too soon.
If my love were for the dead,
Desire would restore
Me to my life again.

My love is for the living;
They point me down to death,
And death I will not take.
My promises have grown,
My kiss was never false,
The faint clear-colored walls
Are not forever down.

BUBBLE OF AIR

The bubbles in the blood sprang free,
crying from roots, from Darwin's beard.
The angel of the century
stood on the night and would be heard;
turned to my dream of tears and sang:
Woman, American, and Jew,
three guardians watch over you,
three lions of heritage
resist the evil of your age:
life, freedom, and memory.
And all the dreams cried from the camps
and all the steel of torture rang.
The angel of the century
stood on the night and cried the great
notes Give Create and Fight—
while war
runs through your veins, while life
a bubble of air stands in your throat,
answer the silence of the weak:
Speak!

LETTER TO THE FRONT

1

Women and poets see the truth arrive.
Then it is acted out,
The lives are lost, and all the newsboys shout.

Horror of cities follows, and the maze
Of compromise and grief.
The feeble cry Defeat be my belief.

All the strong agonized men
Wear the hard clothes of war,
Try to remember what they are fighting for.

But in dark weeping helpless moments of peace
Women and poets believe and resist forever:
The blind inventor finds the underground river.

2

Even during war, moments of delicate peace
Arrive; ceaseless the water ripples, love

Speaks through the river in its human voices.
Through every power to affirm and heal
The unknown world suggests the air and golden
Familiar flowers, and the brief glitter of waves,
And dreams, and leads me always to the real.
Even among these calendars of fire.

Sings: There is much to fear, but not our power.
The stars turn over us; let us not fear the many.
All mortal intricacies tremble upon this flower.
Let us not fear the hidden.   Or each other.
We are alive in an hour whose burning face
Looks into our death, death of our dear wish.
And time that will be eating away our flesh
Gives us this moment when blue settles on rose
And evening suddenly seems limitless silver.
The cold wind streaming over the cold hill-grasses
Remembers and remembers.   Mountains lift into night.
And I am remembering the face of peace.

I have seen a ship lying upon the water
Rise like a great bird, like a lifted promise.

3

They called us to a change of heart
But it was not enough.
Not half enough, not half enough
For all their bargaining and their art.

After the change of heart there comes
The savage waste of battlefield;
The flame of that wild battlefield
Rushes in fire through our rooms.

The heart that comes to know its war
When gambling powers try for place
Must live to wrestle for a place
For every burning human care:

To know a war begins the day
Ideas of peace are bargained for.
Surrender and death are bargained for—
Peace and belief must fight their way.

Begin the day we change and so
Open the spirit to the world.
Wars of the spirit in the world

Make us continually know
We fight continually to grow.

4 Sestina

Coming to Spain on the first day of the fighting,
Flame in the mountains, and the exotic soldiers,
I gave up ideas of strangeness, but now, keeping
All I profoundly hoped for, I saw fearing
Travelers and the unprepared and the fast-changing
Foothills.   The train stopped in a silver country.

Coast-water lit the valleys of this country—
All mysteries stood human in the fighting.
We came from far.   We wondered, Were they changing,
Our mild companions, turning into soldiers?
But the cowards were persistent in their fearing,
Each of us narrowed to one wish he was keeping.

There was no change of heart here; we were keeping
Our deepest wish, meeting with hope this country.
The enemies among us went on fearing
The frontier was too far behind.   This fighting
Was clear to us all at last.   The belted soldiers
Vanished into white hills that dark was changing.

The train stood naked in flowery midnight changing
All complex marvellous hope to war, and keeping
Among us only the main wish, and the soldiers.
We loved each other, believed in the war; this country
Meant to us the arrival of the fighting
At home; we began to know what we were fearing.

As continents broke apart, we saw our fearing
Reflect our nations' fears; we acted as changing
Cities at home would act, with one wish, fighting
This threat or falling under it; we were keeping
The knowledge of fiery promises; this country
Struck at our lives, struck deeper than its soldiers.

Those who among us were sure became our soldiers.
The dreams of peace resolved our subtle fearing.
This was the first day of war in a strange country.
Free Catalonia offered that day our changing
Age's hope and resistance, held in its keeping
The war this age must win in love and fighting.
This first day of fighting showed us all men as soldiers.
It offered one wish for keeping.   Hope.   Deep fearing.
Our changing spirits awake in the soul's country.

5

Much later, I lie in a white seaport night
Of gongs and mystery and bewildered mist
Giving me a strange harbor in these white
Scenes, white rivers, my white dreams of peace.
And a ship lifted up on a sign of freedom.
Peace sharp and immediate as our winter stars.
A blue sailor with a cargo of guitars.

I saw a white ship rise as peace was made
In Spain, the first peace the world would not keep.
The ship pulled away from the harbor where Columbus
Standing on his black pillar sees new worlds;
And suddenly all the people at all the rails
Lifted their hands in a gesture of belief
That climbs among my dreams like a bird flying.
Until the world is lifted by one bird flying
An instant drawing to itself the world.

6

Home thoughts from home; we read you every day,
Soldiers of distances.   You wish most to be here.

In the strange lands of war, I woke and thought of home.
Remembering how war came, I wake and think of you,
In the city of water and stone where I was born,
My home of complex light.   What we were fighting for,
In the beginning, in Spain, was not to be defined.
More human than abstract, more direction than end.
Terror arrived intact, lit with the tragic fire
Of hope before its time, tore us from lover and friend.
We came to the violent act with all that we had learned.

But now we are that home you dream across a war.
You fight; and we must go in poetry and hope
Moving into the future that no one can escape.
Peace will in time arrive, but war defined our years.
We are like that young saint at the spring who bent
Her face over dry earth the vision told her flowed,
Miring herself.   She knew it was water.   But for
Herself, it was filth.   Later, for all to come
Following her faith, miraculous crystal ran.

O saint, O poet, O wounded of these wars
To find life flowing from the heart of man.
We hold belief.   You fight and are maimed and mad.
We believe, though all you want be bed with one
Whose mouth is bread and wine, whose flesh is home.

7

To be a Jew in the twentieth century
Is to be offered a gift.   If you refuse,
Wishing to be invisible, you choose
Death of the spirit, the stone insanity.
Accepting, take full life.   Full agonies:
Your evening deep in labyrinthine blood
Of those who resist, fail, and resist; and God
Reduced to a hostage among hostages.

The gift is torment.   Not alone the still
Torture, isolation; or torture of the flesh.
That may come also.   But the accepting wish,
The whole and fertile spirit as guarantee
For every human freedom, suffering to be free,
Daring to live for the impossible.

8

Evening, bringing me out of the government building,
Spills her blue air, her great Atlantic clouds
Over my hair, reminds me of my land.
My back to high stone and that man's golden bands

Who said of our time which has only its freedom,
"I will not ever say 'for a free world,'
'A better world' or whatever it is;
A man fights to win a war,
To hang on to what is his—"
Consider this man in the clothes of a commander.
Remember that his field is bottled fizz.

O the blue air and the nightsound of heartbeats—
Planes or poems or dreams direct as prayer.
The belief in the world, and we can stand with them,
Whoever clearly fights the order of despair.
In spite of the fascist, Malicioso King,
Contractor, business man and publisher,
Who will hire a man to hire another man
To hire someone to murder the man of strong belief.
Look at him at the Radio City bar;
Remember that he functions best as thief.

O the clouds and the towers are not enough to hide
The little sneer at freedom, the whisper that art died.
Here is the man who changed his name, the man who dyed his hair;
One praises only his own birth; one only his own whore.
Unable to create or fight or commit suicide,
Will make a job of weakness, be the impotent editor,

The sad and pathic bull always wishing he were
The bullfighter.   But we remember the changes that he made,
Screaming "Betrayed!" He forever betrays.   He alone is betrayed.

They are all here in this divided time:
Dies the inquisitor against the truth,
Wheeler, Nye, Pegler, Hearst, each with his crews,
McCormick, the Representatives whose crime
Is against history, the state, and love.
I hold their dead skulls in my hand; this death
Worked against labor, women, Jews,
Reds, Negroes.   But our freedom lives
To fight the war the world must win.
The fevers of confusion's touch
Leap to confusion in the land.
We shall grow and fight again.
The sickness of our divided state
Calls to the anger and the great
Imaginative gifts of man.
The enemy does his rigid work.
We live fighting in that dark.
Let all the living fight in proof
They start the world this war must win.

9

Among all the waste there are the intense stories
And tellers of stories.   One saw a peasant die.
One guarded a soldier through disease.   And one
Saw all the women look at each other in hope.
And came back, saying, "All things must be known."

They come home to the rat-faced investigator
Who sneers and asks, "Who is your favorite poet?"
Voices of scissors and grinders asking their questions:
"How did you ever happen to be against fascism?"
And they remember the general's white hair,
The food-administrator, alone and full of tears.

They come home to the powder-plant at twilight,
The girls emerging like discolored shadows.
But this is a land where there is time, and time;
This is the country where there is time for thinking.
"Is he a 'fellow-traveler'?— No. —Are you sure? —No."
The fear.   Voices of clawhammers and spikes clinking.

If they bomb the cities, they must offer the choice.
Taking away the sons, they must create a reason.
The cities and women cry in a frightful voice,

"I care not who makes the laws, let me make the sons."
But look at their eyes, like drinking animals'
Full of assurance and flowing with reward.
The seeds of answering are in their voice.
The spirit lives, against the time's disease.
You little children, come down out of your mothers
And tell us about peace.

I hear the singing of the lives of women,
The clear mystery, the offering and pride.
But here also the orange lights of a bar, and an
Old biddy singing inside:

> Rain and tomorrow more
> They say there will be rain
> They lean together and tell
> The sorrow of the loin.

> Telling each other, saying
> "But can you understand?"
> They recount separate sorrows.
> Throat.   Forehead.   Hand.

> On the bars and walls of buildings
> They passed when they were young

They vomit out their pain,
The sorrow of the lung.

Who would suspect it of women?
They have not any rest.
Sad dreams of the belly, of the lip,
Of the deep warm breast.

All sorrows have their place in flesh,
All flesh will with its sorrow die—
All but the patch of sunlight over,
Over the sorrowful sunlit eye.

10

Surely it is time for the true grace of women
Emerging, in their lives' colors, from the rooms, from the harvests,
From the delicate prisons, to speak their promises.
The spirit's dreaming delight and the fluid senses'
Involvement in the world.   Surely the day's beginning
In midnight, in time of war, flickers upon the wind.

O on the wasted midnight of our pain
Remember the wasted ones, lost as surely as soldiers
Surrendered to the barbarians, gone down under centuries

Of the starved spirit, in desperate mortal midnight
With the pure throats and cries of blessing, the clearest
Fountains of mercy and continual love.

These years know separation.   O the future shining
In far countries or suddenly at home in a look, in a season,
In music freeing a new myth among the male
Steep landscapes, the familiar cliffs, trees, towers
That stand and assert the earth, saying: "Come here, come to me.
Here are your children."   Not as traditional man
But love's great insight—"your children and your song."

Coming close to the source of belief, these have created
Resistance, the flowering fire of memory,
Given the bread and the dance and the breathing midnight.
Nothing has been begun.   No peace, no word of marvellous
Possible hillsides, the warm lips of the living
Who fought for the spirit's grace among despair,
Beginning with signs of belief, offered in time of war,
As I now send you, for a beginning, praise.

THE SOUL AND BODY OF JOHN BROWN

Multitudes, multitudes in the valley of decision!
    Joel III: 14

His life is in the body of the living.
When they hanged him the first time, his image leaped
into the blackened air.   His grave was the floating faces
of the crowd, and he refusing them release
rose open-eyed in autumn, a fanatic
beacon of fierceness leaping to meet them there,
match the white prophets of the storm,
the streaming meteors of the war.

      Dreaming Ezekiel, threaten me alive!

      Voices: Why don't you rip up that guitar?
      Or must we listen to those blistering strings?

The trial of heroes follows their execution.   The striding
wind of nations with new rain, new lightning,
destroyed in magnificent noon shining straight down
the fiery pines.   Brown wanted freedom.   Could not himself be free

until more grace reached a corroded world   Our guilt his own.
Under the hooded century drops the trap—
There in October's fruition-fire three
tall images of him, Brown as he stood on the ground,
Brown as he stood on sudden air, Brown
standing to our fatal topmost hills
faded through dying altitudes, and low
through faces living under the dregs of the air,
deprived childhood and thwarted youth and change:
       fantastic sweetness gone to rags
       and incorruptible anger blurred by age.

Compel the steps of lovers, watch them lie silvery
attractive in naked embrace over the brilliant gorge,
and open them to love: enlarge their welcome
to sharp-faced countrysides, vicious familiar windows
whose lopped-off worlds say *I am promise*, holding
stopgap slogans of a thin season's offering,
false initials, blind address, dummy name—
enemies who reply in smiles; mild slavers; moderate whores.
There is another gorge to remember, where soldiers give
terrible answers of lechery after death.
Brown said at last, with a living look,
"I designed to have done the same thing
again on a larger scale."   Brown sees his tree

grow in the land to leap these mountains.
Not mountains, but men and women sleeping.

        O my scene! My mother!
        America who offers many births.

Over the tier of barriers, compel the connected steps
past the attacks of sympathy, past black capitals,
to arrive with horizon sharpness, marching
in quick embrace toward people
faltering among hills among the symptoms of ice,
small lights of the shifting winter, the rapid snow-blue stars.
This must be done by armies.   Nothing is free.
Brown refuses to speak direct again,
        "If I tell them the truth,
        they will say I speak in symbols."

White landscapes emphasize his nakedness
reflected in counties of naked who shiver at fires,
their backs to the hands that unroll worlds around them.
They go down the valleys.   They shamble in the streets,
Blind to the sun-storming image in their eyes.
They dread the surface of their victim life,
lying helpless and savage in shade parks,
        asking the towers only what beggars dare:
        food, fire, water, and air.

Spring: the great hieroglyph : the mighty, whose first hour
collects the winter invalids, whose cloudless
pastures train swarms of mutable apple-trees
to blond delusions of light, the touch of whiter
more memorable breasts each evening, the resistant
male shoulders riding under sold terrible eyes.
The soldier-face persists, the victorious head
asks, kissing those breasts, more miracles—
Untarnished hair!   Set them free!   "Without the snap of a gun—"
More failures—but the season is a garden after sickness;
          Then the song begins,
          "The clearing of the sky
          brings fulness to heroes—
          Call Death out of the city
          and ring the summer in."

Whether they sleep alone.   Whether they understand darkness
of mine or tunnel or store.   Whether they lay branches
with skill to entice their visions out of fire.
Whether she lie awake, whether he walk in guilt
down padded corridors, leaving no fingerprints.
Whether he weaken searching for power in papers,
or shut out every fantasy but the fragile eyelid to
          commemorate delight . . .
          They believe in their dreams.

They more and more, secretly, tell their dreams.
They listen oftener for certain words, look deeper
in faces for features of one remembered image.
They almost forget the face.   They cannot miss the look.
It waits until faces have gathered darkness,
and country guitars a wide and subtle music.
It rouses love.   It has mastered its origin:
        Death was its method.   It will surpass its
        furious birth when it is known again.

        Dreaming Ezekiel, threaten me alive!

Greengrown with sun on it.   All the living summer.
They tell their dreams on the cool hill reclining
after a twilight daytime painting machines on the sky,
the spite of tractors and the toothless cannon.
Slaves under factories deal out identical
gestures of reaching—cathedral-color-rose
resumes the bricks as the brick walls lean
away from the windows, blank in bellwavering air,
a slave's mechanical cat's-claw reaping sky.
The cities of horror are down.   These are called born,
and Hungry Hill is a farm again.

I know your face, deepdrowned
prophet, and seablown eyes.

Darkflowing peoples.   A tall tree, prophet, fallen,
your arms in their flesh laid on the mountains, all
your branches in the scattered valleys down.
Your boughs lie broken in channels of the land,
dim anniversaries written on many clouds.
There is no partial help.   Lost in the face of a child,
lost in the factory repetitions, lost
on the steel plateaus, in a ghost distorted.
Calling More Life.   In all the harm calling.
Pointing disaster of death and lifting up the bone,
heroic drug and the intoxication gone.

I see your mouth calling
before the words arrive.

Buzz of guitars repeat it in streamy
summernoon song, the whitelight of the meaning
changed to demand.   More life, challenging
this hatred, this Hallelloo—risk it upon yourselves.
Free all the dangers of promise, clear the image
of freedom for the body of the world.
After the tree is fallen and has become the land,

when the hand in the earth declined rises and touches and
after the walls go down and all the faces turn,
the diamond shoals of eyes demanding life
deep in the prophet eyes, a wish to be again
threatened alive, in agonies of decision
part of our nation of our fanatic sun.

THIS PLACE IN THE WAYS

Having come to this place
I set out once again
on the dark and marvelous way
from where I began:
belief in the love of the world,
woman, spirit, and man.

Having failed in all things
I enter a new age
seeing the old ways as toys,
the houses of a stage
painted and long forgot;
and I find love and rage.

Rage for the world as it is
but for what it may be
more love now than last year
and always less self-pity
since I know in a clearer light
the strength of the mystery.

And at this place in the ways
I wait for song.
My poem-hand still, on the paper,
all night long.
Poems in throat and hand, asleep,
and my storm beating strong!

THEN I SAW WHAT THE CALLING WAS

All the voices of the wood called "Muriel!"
but it was soon solved;   it was nothing, it was not for me.
The words were a little like Mortal and More and Endure
and a word like Real, a sound like Health or Hell.
Then I saw what the calling was : it was the road I traveled, the clear
time and these colors of orchards, gold behind gold and the full
shadow behind each tree and behind each slope.   Not to me
the calling, but to anyone, and at last I saw : where
the road lay through sunlight and many voices and the marvel
orchards, not for me, not for me, not for me.
I came into my clear being;   uncalled, alive, and sure.
Nothing was speaking to me, but I offered and all was well.

And then I arrived at the powerful green hill.

PRIVATE LIFE OF THE SPHINX

for Ella Winter

1

Simply because of a question, my life is implicated:
my flesh and answer fly between chaos and their need.
On the rock I asked the shaky king
one foolish question to make him look at himself—
He looked.   Beheld himself and kingdoms.   Took.
My claws and smile transferred into his myth.

Babble of demand, and answers building the brilliant cities
the standing battlefields and the fields of the fallen down.

Now in this city in the Lounge of Time,
I tell you it was a legend founded on fire,
founded on what we are.   Simply because I asked one question,
"What is this, What?"   so that the answer must be "Man."
Because of that they bring their riddles and rhyme
to my door if I houseless run throughout the world,
torse of a woman and quarters of a lion.

2

Open war with its images of love and death—
man, an explosion walking through the night in
rich and intolerable loneliness.
Cathedrals writhing gold against their clouds
and a child asking the fiery pure questions.
The monkey-dark, a month of smoky violets,
delicate repose of my reality among
dreams, and the angel of the resurrection,
a mouth overhead, the sky planted with stars.

My questions are my body.   And among this glowing, this
sure, this fact, this mooncolored breast, I make memorial.

3

My body is set against disorder.   Risen among enigmas,
time and the question carry a rose of form,
sing a life-song.   Strangler and bitch, they said,
but they mistook the meaning of my name:
I am the root who embraces and the source.
I sing.   I sing.

In these cities, all suffer from their weaknesses—
they lack some gut, they are ill, they have womb-envy,
run howling from the question and the act.
They bring me their need for answers in their hands and eyes.
To embody truth, the Irish old man said.

I remember in Calabria a peasant
broad, smiling, and sly, with a bird throbbing and small
behind his back, in his hands;   and he asked his question.
Is it alive? and he smiled at me.   Then I knew
if I said Yes, he would twist the sparrow's neck.
The fool of time!   I gave him my only answer,
that answer of time:
Fool, I said, you know it depends on you
whether it live or die.

4

I answer!   I fly reborn from deep escape!
Listen to their cries, the selfsame crying throats,
crying the selfsame need.
Here is my self.   I touch you, life reaches me.
You touch me, I am able to give my gifts.
All the acts flow together, a form being made.
I know a garden beyond questioning—

can almost see night-flowering white mallows,
can almost tell you below the sound of water,
white lilac like a voluptuous light
shining at full on our two faces—
It goes ahead of our hope.   It is the secret that moves
with the speed of life,
     secrets of night and   the street
secrets of milk and dinner and daylight,
enigmas of gardens, the kitchen and the bed,
the riddle and sacrament in the knot of wood,
in the wine, in the water and root the coil of life.

They ask for answers, they starving eat their shadows.
The beginning is always here.   Its green demand.

5

They think I answer and strangle.   They are wrong.
I set my life among the questioning.
The peasant, the wars, the wounded powerful king.
The shining of questions which cannot be concealed
lies in that mirror.   The little child to the mother
of the father's unspoken death, said : "You have told me
     yourself."

Even alone, away from daily life, the fire
and monster crown of the legend over me
reaches their eyes—children, friendship of lions,
the sense of the world at last broken through to man
in all fury, all sacred open mystery,
is in my question.

                  The stranger, the foreign and strong,
the child and king, wide village eyes of the farm,
the demand loud, or choking in surf-foam,
density of flowers, the faces of all love,
the core of our hope;   stronger than kill,
stronger almost than question, almost than song.

FOURTH ELEGY. THE REFUGEES

And the child sitting alone planning her hope:
I want to write for my race.   But what race will you speak,
being American?   I want to write for the living.
But the young grow more around us every day.
They show new faces, they come from far, they live
occupied with escape, freeze in the passes, sail
early in the morning.   A few arrive to help.
          Mother, those were not angels, they were knights.

Many are cast out, become artists at rejection.
They saw the chute, the intelligible world
so wild become, it fell, a hairy apparent star
this time with not a public saint in sight
to record miracle.   The age of the masked and the alone begins,
we look for sinister states, a loss shall learning suffer
before the circle of this sun be done,
the palace birds of the new tyrants rise
flying into the wounded sky, sky of catastrophe;
help may be near, but remedy is far,
rain, blood, milk, famine, iron, and epidemic
pour in the sky where a comet drags his tail.
The characters of the spectacles are dead,

nothing is left but ventriloquists and children,
and bodies without souls are not a sacrifice.

It is the children's voyage must be done
before the refugees come home again.
They run like lemmings out
building their suffocated bodies up
to let the full stream pass.
The predatory birds sail over them.
They dash themselves into lighthouses, where the great
        lights hold up,
they laugh at sympathy: "Have you nothing better to do
        in the trenches?"
And at that brink, that bending over doom,
become superior to themselves, in crisis.
There is an addition and fusion of qualities.

They are the children.   They have their games.
They made a circle on a map of time,
skipping they entered it, laughing lifted the agate.
I will get you an orange cat, and a pig called Tangerine.
The gladness-bird beats wings against an opaque glass.
There is a white bird in the top of the tree.
They leave their games, and pass.

Cut.   Frozen and cut.   Off at the ankle.   Off at the hip.
            Off at the knee.   Cut off.
Crossing the mountains many died of cold.

We have spoken of guilt to you too long.
The blame grows on us who carry you the news.
And as the man bringing the story of suicide
lives with the fact, feels murder in himself,
as murderous regents with their gentle kings
know the seductions of crime long before death takes hold,
we bear their—
                        a child crying shrill in a white street
"Aviación!" among the dust of geysers,
the curling rust of Spanish tile.
We bear their smile, we smile under the guilt,
in an access of sickness, "Let me alone, I'm healthy!"
cry. And in danger, the sexually witty
speak in short sentences, the unfulfilled.
While definition levels others out.
Wish : the unreality of fulfilled action.
Wish : the reality of fulfilled thought.
Images of luxury.   Image of life.
A phoenix at play among the peonies.
The random torture predicts the random thought.
Over the thought and bird and flowers, the plane.

Coming to strange countries refugee children find
land burned over by winter, a white field and black star
falling like firework where no rockets are
into hell-cities with blank brick and church-bells
(I like this city.   This is a peaceful city)
ringing the bees in the hot garden with their mixing sounds,
ringing the love that falters among these hills,
red-flowering maple and the laugh of peace.
It will take a bell-ringing god tremendous imagined descending
for the healing of hell.

A line of birds, a line of gods.   Of bells.
And all the birds have settled on their shadows.
And down the shadowed street a line of children.
You can make out the child ahead of you.
It turns with a gesture that asks for a soft answer.
It sees the smaller child ahead of it.
The child ahead of it turns.   Now, in the close-up
faces throw shadow off.   It is yourself
walks down this street at five-year intervals,
seeing yourself diminishing ahead,
five years younger, and five years younger, and young,
until the farthest infant has a face
ready to grow into any child in the world.

They take to boats.   The shipwreck of New York.
To trains whose sets of lines pass along boxes,
children's constructions.
Rush to rejection
foreknowing the steps,

>disfigurement of women, insults of disease,
>negations of power.   They people the earth.
>They are the strong.   They see the enemy.
>They dream the relaxed heart, coming again to power,
>the struggle, the Milk-Tree of Children's Paradise.

They are the real creation of a fictional character.
They fuse a dead world straight.
A line of shadowy children issues, surf issues it,
sickness boiled in their flesh, but they are whole,
insular strength surrounds them, hunger feeds them strong,
the ripened sun finds them, they are the first of the world,
free of the ferryman Nostalgia, who stares at the backward shore.
Growing free of the old in their slow growth of death,
they hold the flaming apples of the spring.
They are exposed to danger.
Ledges of water trick them,
they fall through the raw colors of excavations,
are crushed by monuments, high stone like whale-blow rising,
the backwash of machines can strike them down.

A hill on a map claims them, their procession reaches
a wavy topographical circle where
two gunners lie behind their steelwork margins,
spray shot across the line, do random death.
They fire in a world infected by trenches,
through epidemics of injuries, Madrid, Shanghai,
Vienna, Barcelona, all cities of contagion,
issue survivors from the surf of the age.
Free to be very hungry and very lonely.
And in the countries of the mind, Cut off at the knee.   Cut off at the
     armpit.   Cut off at the throat.
Free to reclaim the world and sow a legend,
to make the adjustments never made,
repair the promises broken and the promise kept.
They blame our lives, lie on our wishes with their eyes our own,
to say and to remember and avenge.   A lullaby for a believing child.

EIGHTH ELEGY. CHILDREN'S ELEGY

Yes, I have seen their eyes.   In peaceful gardens
the dark flowers now are always children's eyes,
full-colored, haunted as evening under fires
showered from the sky of a burning country.

Shallow-featured children under trees
look up among green shadows of the leaves.
The angel, flaming, gives—into his hands
all is given and he does not change.
The child changes and takes.

All is given.   He makes and changes.
The angel stands.

A flame over the tree.   Night calling in the cloud.
And shadow among winds.   Where does the darkness lie?
It comes out of the person, says the child.
A shadow tied and alive, trying to be.

In the tremendous child-world, everything is high,
active and fiery, sun-cats run through the walls,
the tree blows overhead like a green joy,
and cloudy leopards go hunting in the sky.

The shadow in us sings, "Stand out of the light!"
But I live, I live, I travel in the sun.

❧

On burning voyages of war they go.
Like starving ghosts they stumble after nuns.
Children of heroes, Defeat the dark companion.
But if they are told they are happy, they will know.

Who kills the father burns up the children's tears.
Some suffering blazes beyond all human touch,
some sounds of suffering cry, far out of reach.
These children bring to us their mother's fears.

Singing, "O make us strong O let us go—"
The new world comes among the old one's harms,
old world carrying new world in her arms.
But if you say they are free, then they will know.

War means to me, sings a small skeleton,
only the separation,
mother no good and gone,
taken away in lines of fire and foam.
The end of war
will bring me, bring me home.

The children of the defeated, sparrow-poor and starved,
create, create, must make their world again.
Dead games and false salutes must be their grace.

One wish must move us, flicker from our lives
to the marred face.

My child, my victim, my wish this moment come!
But the martyr-face cries to us fiercely
"I search to learn the way out of childhood;
I need to fight.   I wish, I wish for home."

෴

This is what they say, who were broken off from love:
However long we were loved, it was not long enough.

We were afraid of the broad big policeman,
of lions and tigers, the dark hall and the moon.

After our father went, nothing was ever the same,
when mother did not come back, we made up a war game.

My cat was sitting in the doorway when the planes
went over, and my cat saw mother cry;
furry tears, fire fell, wall went down;
did my cat see mother die?

Mother is gone away, my cat sits here coughing.
I cough and sit.   I am nobody's nothing.

However long they loved us, it was not long enough.
For we have to be strong, to know what they did, and then
our people are saved in time, our houses built again.

You will not know, you have a sister and brother;
my doll is not my child, my doll is my mother.

However strong we are, it is not strong enough.
I want to grow up.   To come back to love.

      ❧

I see it pass before me in parade,
my entire life as a procession of images.
The toy, the golden kernel, the glass lamp.
The present she gave me, the first page I read,
the little animal, the shadowless tall angel.
The angel stands.   The child changes and takes.
He makes a world, stands up among the cousins,
cries to the family, "Ladies and gentlemen—
The world is falling *down!*"   After the smooth hair
darkens, and summer lengthens the smooth cheek,
and the diffuse gestures are no longer weak,
he begins to be the new one, to have what happened,
to do what must be done.

O, when the clouds and the blue horse of childhood
melt away and the golden weapons,
and we remember the first public day's
drums and parades and the first angel
standing in the garden, his dark lips
and silver blood, how he stood,
giving, for all he was given.

I begin to have what happened to me.

O, when the music of carousels and stars
is known, and the music of the scene
makes a clear meeting, greeting and claim of gods,
we see through the hanging curtain of the year
they change each other with one change of love!
see, in one breath, in a look!
See, in pure midnight a flare of broken color
clears to a constellation.
Peace is asleep, war's lost.   It is love.
I wanted to die.   The masked and the alone
seemed the whole world, and all the gods at war,
and all the people dead and depraved.   Today
the constellation and the music!   Love.

You who seeking yourself arrive at these lines,

look once, and you see the world,
look twice and you see your self.

And all the children moving in their change.

To have what has happened, the pattern and the shock;
and all of them walk out of their childhood,
give to you one blue look.

And all the children bowing in their game,
saying Farewell, Goodbye; Goodbye, Farewell.

HAYING BEFORE STORM

This sky is unmistakable. Not lurid, not low, not black.
Illuminated and bruise-color, limitless, to the noon
Full of its floods to come. Under it, field, wheels, and mountain,
The valley scattered with friends, gathering in
Live-colored harvest, filling their arms; not seeming to hope
Not seeming to dread, doing.
                     I stand where I can see
Holding a small pitcher, coming in toward
The doers and the day.
                     These images are all
Themselves emerging: they face their moment: love or go down,
A blade of the strong hay stands like light before me.
The sky is a torment on our eyes, the sky
Will not wait for this golden, it will not wait for form.
There is hardly a moment to stand before the storm.
There is hardly time to lay hand to the great earth.
Or time to tell again what power shines past storm.

KING'S MOUNTAIN

In all the cities of this year
I have longed for the other city.

In all the rooms of this year
I have entered one red room.

In all the futures I have walked toward
I have seen a future I can hardly name.

But here the road we drive
Turns upon another country.

I have seen white beginnings,
A slow sea without glaze or speed,
Movement of land, a long lying-down dance.

This is fog-country. Milk. Country of time.

I see your tormented color, the steep front of your storm
Break dissipated among limitless profiles.

I see the shapes of waves in the cross-sea
Advance, a fog-surface over the fog-floor.
Seamounts, slow-flowing. Color. Plunge-point of air.

In all the meanings of this year
There will be the ferny meaning.

It rises leaning and green, streams through star-lattices;
After the last cliff, wave-eroded silver,
Forgets the limitations of our love,
These drifts and caves dissolve and pillars of these countries
Long-crested dissolve to the future, a new form.

F. O. M.

The Death of Matthiessen

It was much stronger than they said. Noisier.
Everything in it more colored. Wilder.
More at the center calm.
Everything was more violent than ever they said,
Who tried to guard us from suicide and life.
We in our wars were more than they had told us.
Now that descent figures stand about the horizon,
I have begun to see the living faces,
The storm, the morning, all more than they ever said.
Of the new dead, that friend who died today,
Angel of suicides, gather him in now.
Defend us from doing what he had to do
Who threw himself away.

POURING MILK AWAY

Here, again. A smell of dying in the milk-pale carton,
And nothing then but pour the milk away.
More of the small and killed, the child's, wasted,
Little white arch of the drink and taste of day.
Spoiled, gone and forgotten; thrown away.

Day after day I do what I condemned in countries.
Look, the horror, the waste of food and bone.
You will know why when you have lived alone.

[UNTITLED]

The power of war leads to a plan of lives
Involving rivers. The many-stated million
Human concerns. This touches, this gives life
To all its forms. Now clothe our force,
Make it as flexible as a man venturing
To fend for himself in his own enterprise.

Now in the unity of all vision, unity of the land, the forests
    and water,
See nature, the nation, as a web of lives
On the earth together, full of their potencies.
The total unity, reached past images,
Reaching past the naming of religions.
We reach to create. That is our central meaning,
Suggestion of art and altar in all our passwords,
For the meaning of "mirror of nature," the meaning of "image
    of God"
Is a simple fiery meaning : man is to create.
Making, singing, bring the potential to day.

[UNTITLED]

A tree of rivers flowing through our lives;
These lives moving through their starvation and greatness,
Masked away from each other, masked in lack.
Each woman seen as a river through whom lifetime
Gives, and feeds. Each man seen giving and feeding.
Under all the images, under all growth and form. The energy
      of each, which is relation,
A flare of linked fire which is the need to grow,
The human wish for meaning.
                        Roots of diversity
Each being witness to itself, entering to relate,
Bearing the flood, the food, the becoming of power,
Which is our eyes and our lives
Related, in bonds of flow.

[UNTITLED]

On your journey you will come to a time of waking.
The others may be asleep. Or you may be alone.

Immediacy of song moving the titled
Visions of children and the linking stars.

You will begin then to remember. You
Hear the voice relating after late listening.

You remember even falling asleep, or a dream of sleep.
For now the song is given and you remember.

At every clear waking you have known this song,
The cities of this music identified

By the white springs of singing, and their fountains
Reflected in windows, in all the human eyes.

The wishes, the need growing. The song growing.

TO ENTER THAT RHYTHM WHERE
THE SELF IS LOST

To enter that rhythm where the self is lost,
where breathing : heartbeat : and the subtle music
of their relation make our dance, and hasten
us to the moment when all things become
magic, another possibility.
That blind moment, midnight, when all sight
begins, and the dance itself is all our breath,
and we ourselves the moment of life and death.
Blinded;   but given now another saving,
the self as vision, at all times perceiving,
all arts all senses being languages,
delivered of will, being transformed in truth—
for life's sake surrendering moment and images,
writing the poem;   in love making;   bringing to birth.

THE POEM AS MASK

Orpheus

When I wrote of the women in their dances and wildness,
　　　　it was a mask,
on their mountain, god-hunting, singing, in orgy,
it was a mask; when I wrote of the god,
fragmented, exiled from himself, his life, the love gone
　　　　　down with song,
it was myself, split open, unable to speak, in exile from
　　　　myself.

There is no mountain, there is no god, there is memory
of my torn life, myself split open in sleep, the rescued child
beside me among the doctors, and a word
of rescue from the great eyes.

No more masks! No more mythologies!

Now, for the first time, the god lifts his hand,
the fragments join in me with their own music.

IN OUR TIME

In our period, they say there is free speech.
They say there is no penalty for poets,
There is no penalty for writing poems.
They say this.   This is the penalty.

THE OVERTHROW OF ONE O'CLOCK
AT NIGHT

is my concern.   That's this moment,
when I lean on my elbows out the windowsill
and feel the city among its time-zones, among its seas,
among its late night news, the pouring in
of everything meeting, wars, dreams, winter night.
Light in snowdrifts causing the young girls
lying awake to fall in love tonight
alone in bed; or the little children
half world over tonight rained on by fire—that's us—
calling on somebody—that's us—to come
and help them.

             Now I see at the boundary of darkness
extreme of moonlight.

                    Alone.   All my hopes
scattered in people quarter world away
half world away, out of all hearing.

                       Tell myself:
Trust in experience.   And in the rhythms.
The deep rhythms of your experience.

SONG : LOVE IN WHOSE RICH HONOR

Love
in whose rich honor
I stand looking from my window
over the starved trees of a dry September
Love
deep and so far forbidden
is bringing me
a gift
to claw at my skin
to break open my eyes
the gift longed for so long
The power
to write
out of the desperate ecstasy at last
death and madness

NIOBE NOW

Niobe
>   wild
>   with unbelief
>   as all
>   her ending
>   turns to stone

Not gentle
>   weeping
>   and souvenirs
>   but hammering
>   honking
>   agonies

Forty-nine tragic years
>   are done
>   and the twentieth century
>   not begun:

All tears,
>   all tears,
>   all tears.

Water

      from her rock

           is sprung

               and in this water

                    lives a seed

That must endure

          and grow

              and shine

                beasts, gardens

                    at last rivers

A man

      to be born

          to start again

              to tear

                a woman

                    from his side

And wake

      to start

          the world again.

ANEMONE

My eyes are closing, my eyes are opening.
You are looking into me with your waking look.

My mouth is closing, my mouth is opening.
You are waiting with your red promises.

My sex is closing, my sex is opening.
You are singing and offering : the way in.

My life is closing, my life is opening.
You are here.

FOR MY SON

You come from poets, kings, bankrupts, preachers,
        attempted bankrupts, builders of cities, salesmen,
the great rabbis, the kings of Ireland, failed drygoods
        storekeepers, beautiful women of the songs,
great horsemen, tyrannical fathers at the shore of ocean,
        the western mothers looking west beyond from their
            windows,
the families escaping over the sea hurriedly and by night—
the roundtowers of the Celtic violet sunset,
the diseased, the radiant, fliers, men thrown out of town,
        the man bribed by his cousins to stay out of town,
            teachers, the cantor on Friday evening, the lurid
              newspapers,
strong women gracefully holding relationship, the Jewish girl
        going to parochial school, the boys racing their iceboats
            on the Lakes,
the woman still before the diamond in the velvet window,
        saying "Wonder of nature."
Like all men,
you come from singers, the ghettoes, the famines, wars and
        refusal of wars, men who built villages
that grew to our solar cities, students, revolutionists, the
        pouring of buildings, the market newspapers,

a poor tailor in a darkening room,
a wilderness man, the hero of mines, the astronomer, a
    white-faced woman hour on hour teaching piano and
        her crippled wrist,
like all men,
you have not seen your father's face
but he is known to you forever in song, the coast of the skies,
    in dream, wherever you find man playing his
        part as father, father among our light, among our
        darkness,
and in your self made whole, whole with yourself and
    whole with others,
the stars your ancestors.

POEM

I lived in the first century of world wars.
Most mornings I would be more or less insane,
The newspapers would arrive with their careless stories,
The news would pour out of various devices
Interrupted by attempts to sell products to the unseen.
I would call my friends on other devices;
They would be more or less mad for similar reasons.
Slowly I would get to pen and paper,
Make my poems for others unseen and unborn.
In the day I would be reminded of those men and women
Brave, setting up signals across vast distances,
Considering a nameless way of living, of almost unimagined values.
As the lights darkened, as the lights of night brightened,
We would try to imagine them, try to find each other.
To construct peace, to make love, to reconcile
Waking with sleeping, ourselves with each other,
Ourselves with ourselves. We would try by any means
To reach the limits of ourselves, to reach beyond ourselves,
To let go the means, to wake.

I lived in the first century of these wars.

WHAT THEY SAID

: After I am dead, darling,
    my seventeen senses gone,
I shall love you as you wish,
    no sex, no mouth, but bone—
    in the way you long for now,
with my soul alone.

: When we are neither woman nor man
    but bleached to skeleton—
when you have changed, my darling,
    and all your senses gone,
    it is not me that you will love:
you will love everyone.

THE BACKSIDE OF THE ACADEMY

Five brick panels, three small windows, six lions' heads
    with rings in their mouths, five pairs of closed bronze doors—
the shut wall with the words carved across its head
ART REMAINS THE ONE WAY POSSIBLE OF
    SPEAKING TRUTH.—
On this May morning, light swimming in this street,
    the children running,
on the church beside the Academy the lines are flying
of little yellow-and-white plastic flags flapping in the light;
and on the great shut wall, the words are carved across:
WE ARE YOUNG AND WE ARE FRIENDS OF TIME.—
Below that, a light blue asterisk in chalk
and in white chalk, Hector, Joey, Lynn, Rudolfo.
A little up the street, a woman shakes a small dark boy,
she shouts What's wrong with you, ringing that bell!
In the street of rape and singing, poems, small robberies,
carved in an oblong panel of the stone:
CONSCIOUS UTTERANCE OF THOUGHT BY
    SPEECH OR ACTION
TO ANY END IS ART.—
On the lowest reach of the walls are chalked the words:
    Jack is a object,

Walter and Trina, Goo Goo, I love Trina,
and further along Viva Fidel now altered to Muera Fidel.
A deep blue marble is lodged against the curb.
A phone booth on one corner; on the other, the big mesh
          basket for trash.
Beyond them, the little park is always locked. For the two
          soldier brothers.
And past that goes on an eternal football game
which sometimes, as on this day in May, transforms to stickball
as, for one day in May,
five pairs of closed bronze doors will open
and the Academy of writers, sculptors, painters, composers,
          their guests and publishers will all roll in and
the wave of organ music come rolling out into
the street where light now blows and papers and little
          children and words, some breezes of Spanish blow
               and many colors of people.

A watch cap lies fallen against a cellophane which used
          to hold pistachio nuts
and here before me, on my street,
five brick panels, three small windows, six lions' heads with
          rings in their mouths, five pairs of closed bronze doors,
light flooding the street I live and write in; and across the
          river the one word FREE against the ferris wheel and
               the roller coaster,

and here, painted upon the stones, Chino, Bobby, Joey,
    Fatmoma, Willy, Holy of God
and also Margaret is a shit and also fuck and shit;
far up, invisible at the side of the building:
WITHOUT VISION THE PEO
and on the other side, the church side,
where shadows of trees and branches, this day in May, are
    printed balanced on the church wall,
in-focus trunks and softened-focus branches
below the roof where the two structures stand,
bell and cross, antenna and weathervane,
I can see past the church the words of an ending line:
IVE BY BREAD ALONE.

THE FLYING RED HORSE

On all the streetcorners the children are standing,
They ask What can it mean?
The grownups answer   A flying red horse
Signifies gasoline.

The man at the Planetarium,
Pointing beyond the sky,
Is not going to say that Pegasus
Means poetry.

Some of our people feel like death,
And some feel rather worse.
His energy, in this night of lies,
Flies right against the curse.

What's *red?*   What is the *flying horse?*
They swear they do not know,
But just the same, and every night,
All the streetcorners glow.

Even the Pentagon, even the senators,
Even the President sitting on his arse—
Never mind—over all cities
The flying red horse.

KÄTHE KOLLWITZ

1

Held between wars
my lifetime
          among wars, the big hands of the world of death
my lifetime
listens to yours.

The faces of the sufferers
in the street, in dailiness,
their lives showing
through their bodies
a look as of music
the revolutionary look
that says   I am in the world
to change the world
my lifetime
is to love to endure to suffer the music
to set its portrait
up as a sheet of the world
the most moving the most alive
Easter and bone
and Faust walking among flowers of the world

and the child alive within the living woman, music of man,
and death holding my lifetime between great hands
the hands of enduring life
that suffers the gifts and madness of full life, on earth, in our time,
and through my life, through my eyes, through my arms and hands
may give the face of this music in portrait waiting for
the unknown person
held in the two hands, you.

2

Woman as gates, saying :
"The process is after all like music,
like the development of a piece of music.
The fugues come back and

                        again and again
interweave.
A theme may seem to have been put aside,
but it keeps returning—
the same thing modulated,
somewhat changed in form.
Usually richer.
And it is very good that this is so."

A woman pouring her opposites.
"After all there are happy things in life too.
Why do you show only the dark side?"
"I could not answer this. But I know—
in the beginning my impulse to know
the working life

                    had little to do with
pity or sympathy.
                    I simply felt
that the life of the workers was beautiful."

She said, "I am groping in the dark."

She said, "When the door opens, of sensuality,
then you will understand it too. The struggle begins.
Never again to be free of it,
often you will feel it to be your enemy.
Sometimes
you will almost suffocate,
such joy it brings."

Saying of her husband : "My wish
is to die after Karl.
I know no person who can love as he can,
with his whole soul.

Often this love has oppressed me;
I wanted to be free.
But often too it has made me
so terribly happy."

She said : "We rowed over to Carrara at dawn,
climbed up to the marble quarries
and rowed back at night. The drops of water
fell like glittering stars
from our oars."

She said : "As a matter of fact,
I believe
            that bisexuality
is almost   a necessary factor
in artistic production; at any rate,
the tinge of masculinity within me
helped me
            in my work."

She said : "The only technique I can still manage.
It's hardly a technique at all, lithography.
In it
            only the essentials count."

A tight-lipped man in a restaurant last night saying to me :
"Kollwitz?   She's too black-and-white."

3

Held among wars, watching
   all of them
   all these people
   weavers,
   Carmagnole

Looking at
   all of them
   death, the children
   patients in waiting-rooms
   famine
   the street
   the corpse with the baby
   floating, on the dark river

A woman seeing
   the violent, inexorable
   movement of nakedness
   and the confession of No

the confession of great weakness, war,
all streaming to one son killed, Peter;
even the son left living; repeated,
the father, the mother; the grandson
another Peter killed in another war; firestorm;
dark, light, as two hands,
this pole and that pole as the gates.

What would happen if one woman told the truth about her life?
  The world would split open

4 Song : The Calling-Up

Rumor, stir of ripeness
rising within this girl
sensual blossoming
of meaning, its light and form.

The birth-cry summoning
out of the male, the father
from the warm woman
a mother in response.

The word of death
calls up the fight with stone

wrestle with grief with time
from the material make
an art harder than bronze.

5 Self-Portrait

Mouth looking directly at you
eyes in their inwardness looking
directly at you
half light   half darkness
woman, strong, German, young artist
flows into
wide sensual mouth meditating
looking right at you
eyes shadowed with brave hand
looking deep at you
flows into
wounded brave mouth
grieving and hooded eyes
alive, German, in her first War
flows into
strength of the worn face
a skein of lines
broods, flows into
mothers among the war graves

bent over death
facing the father
stubborn upon the field
flows into
the marks of her knowing—
Nie Wieder Krieg
repeated in the eyes
flows into
"Seedcorn must not be ground"
and the grooved cheek
lips drawn fine
the down-drawn grief
face of our age
flows into
Pieta, mother and
between her knees
life as her son in death
pouring from the sky of
one more war
flows into
face almost obliterated
hand over the mouth forever
hand over one eye now
the other great eye
closed

THE SPEED OF DARKNESS

1

Whoever despises the clitoris despises the penis
Whoever despises the penis despises the cunt
Whoever despises the cunt despises the life of the child.

Resurrection music,   silence,   and surf.

2

No longer speaking
Listening with the whole body
And with every drop of blood
Overtaken by silence

But this same silence is become speech
With the speed of darkness.

3

Stillness during war, the lake.
The unmoving spruces.

Glints over the water.
Faces, voices.   You are far away.
A tree that trembles.

I am the tree that trembles and trembles.

4

After the lifting of the mist
after the lift of the heavy rains
the sky stands clear
and the cries of the city risen in day
I remember the buildings are space
walled, to let space be used for living
I mind this room is space
this drinking glass is space
whose boundary of glass
lets me give you drink and space to drink
your hand, my hand being space
containing skies and constellations
your face
carries the reaches of air
I know I am space
my words are air.

5

Between   between
the man : act   exact
woman : in curve   senses in their maze
frail orbits, green tries,   games of stars
shape of the body speaking its evidence

6

I look across at the real
vulnerable   involved   naked
devoted to the present of all I care for
the world of its history leading to this moment.

7

Life the announcer.
I assure you
there are many ways to have a child.
I bastard mother
promise you
there are many ways to be born.
They all come forth
in their own grace.

8

Ends of the earth join tonight
with blazing stars upon their meeting.

These sons,   these sons
fall burning into Asia.

9

Time comes into it.
Say it.   Say it.
The universe is made of stories,
not of atoms.

10

Lying
blazing beside me
you rear beautifully and up—
your thinking face—
erotic body reaching
in all its colors and lights—
your erotic face
colored and lit—

not colored body-and-face
but now entire,
colors   lights   the world thinking and reaching.

11

The river flows past the city.

Water goes down to tomorrow
making its children   I hear their unborn voices
I am working out the vocabulary of my silence.

12

Big-boned man young and of my dream
Struggles to get the live bird out of his throat.
I am he am I?   Dreaming?
I am the bird am I?   I am the throat?

A bird with a curved beak.
It could slit anything, the throat-bird.

Drawn up slowly.   The curved blades, not large.
Bird emerges   wet   being born
Begins to sing.

13

My night awake
staring at the broad rough jewel
the copper roof across the way
thinking of the poet
yet unborn in this dark
who will be the throat of these hours.
No.   Of those hours.
Who will speak these days,
if not I,
if not you?

WAKING THIS MORNING

Waking this morning,
a violent woman in the violent day
Laughing.
                    Past the line of memory
along the long body of your life
in which move childhood, youth, your lifetime of touch,
eyes, lips, chest, belly, sex, legs, to the waves of the sheet.
I look past the little plant
on the city windowsill
to the tall towers bookshaped, crushed together in greed,
the river flashing flowing corroded,
the intricate harbor and the sea, the wars, the moon, the
    planets, all who people space
in the sun visible invisible.
African violets in the light
breathing, in a breathing universe.   I want strong peace,
    and delight,
the wild good.
I want to make my touch poems:
to find my morning, to find you entire
alive moving among the anti-touch people.

I say across the waves of the air to you:
today once more
I will try to be non-violent
one more day
this morning, waking the world away
in the violent day.

WAITING FOR ICARUS

He said he would be back and we'd drink wine together
He said that everything would be better than before
He said we were on the edge of a new relation
He said he would never again cringe before his father
He said that he was going to invent full-time
He said he loved me that going into me
He said was going into the world and the sky
He said all the buckles were very firm
He said the wax was the best wax
He said Wait for me here on the beach
He said Just don't cry

I remember the gulls and the waves
I remember the islands going dark on the sea
I remember the girls laughing
I remember they said he only wanted to get away from me
I remember mother saying : Inventors are like poets,
                                        a trashy lot
I remember she told me those who try out inventions are
    worse

I remember she added: Women who love such are the worst
   of all
I have been waiting all day, or perhaps longer.
I would have liked to try those wings myself.
It would have been better than this.

DESPISALS

In the human cities, never again to
despise the backside of the city, the ghetto,
or build it again as we build the despised
backsides of houses.   Look at your own building.
You are the city.

Among our secrecies, not to despise our Jews
(that is, ourselves) or our darkness, our blacks,
or in our sexuality   wherever it takes us
and we now know we are productive
too productive, too reproductive
for our present invention—never to despise
the homosexual who goes building another

with touch   with touch   (not to despise any touch)
each like himself, like herself each.
You are this.

                                    In the body's ghetto
never to go despising the asshole
nor the useful shit that is our clean clue
to what we need.   Never to despise
the clitoris in her least speech.

Never to despise in myself what I have been taught
to despise.   Not to despise the other.
Not to despise the *it*.   To make this relation
with the it : to know that I am it.

MYTH

Long afterward, Oedipus, old and blinded, walked the
roads.   He smelled a familiar smell.   It was
the Sphinx.   Oedipus said, "I want to ask one question.
Why didn't I recognize my mother?"   "You gave the
wrong answer," said the Sphinx.   "But that was what
made everything possible," said Oedipus.   "No," she said.
"When I asked, What walks on four legs in the morning,
two at noon, and three in the evening, you answered,
Man.   You didn't say anything about woman."
"When you say Man," said Oedipus, "you include women
too. Everyone knows that."   She said, "That's what
you think."

BALLAD OF ORANGE AND GRAPE

After you finish your work
after you do your day
after you've read your reading
after you've written your say—
you go down the street to the hot dog stand,
one block down and across the way.
On a blistering afternoon in East Harlem in the twentieth century.

Most of the windows are boarded up,
the rats run out of a sack—
sticking out of the crummy garage
one shiny long Cadillac;
at the glass door of the drug-addiction center,
a man who'd like to break your back.
But here's a brown woman with a little girl dressed in rose and pink, too.

Frankfurters frankfurters sizzle on the steel
where the hot-dog-man leans—
nothing else on the counter
but the usual two machines,
the grape one, empty, and the orange one, empty,
I face him in between.
A black boy comes along, looks at the hot dogs, goes on walking.

I watch the man as he stands and pours
in the familiar shape
bright purple in the one marked ORANGE
orange in the one marked GRAPE,
the grape drink in the machine marked ORANGE
and orange drink in the GRAPE.
Just the one word large and clear, unmistakable, on each machine.

I ask him : How can we go on reading
and make sense out of what we read?—
How can they write and believe what they're writing,
the young ones across the street,
while you go on pouring grape into ORANGE
and orange into the one marked GRAPE—?
(How are we going to believe what we read and we write
    and we hear and we say and we do?)

He looks at the two machines and he smiles
and he shrugs and smiles and pours again.
It could be violence and nonviolence
it could be white and black   women and men
it could be war and peace or any
binary system, love and hate, enemy, friend.
Yes and no, be and not-be, what we do and what we don't do.

On a corner in East Harlem
garbage, reading, a deep smile, rape,
forgetfulness, a hot street of murder,
misery, withered hope,
a man keeps pouring grape into ORANGE
and orange into the one marked GRAPE,
pouring orange into GRAPE and grape into ORANGE forever.

DON BATY, THE DRAFT RESISTER

I Muriel stood at the altar-table
The young man Don Baty stood with us
I Muriel fell away in me
in dread but in a welcoming
I am Don Baty then I said
before the blue-coated police
ever entered and took him.

I am Don Baty, say we all
we eat our bread, we drink our wine.
Our heritage has come, we know,
your arrest is mine. Yes.
Beethoven saying Amen Amen Amen Amen Amen
and all a singing, earth and eyes,
strong and weaponless.

There is a pounding at the door;
now we bring our lives entire.
I am Don Baty. My dear, my dear,
in a kind of welcoming,
here we meet, here we bring
ourselves. They pound on the wall of time.
The newborn are with us singing.

SECRETS OF AMERICAN CIVILIZATION

for Staughton Lynd

Jefferson spoke of freedom but he held slaves.
Were ten of them his sons by black women?
Did he sell them? or was his land their graves?
Do we asking our questions become more human?

Are our lives the parable which, living,
We all have, we all know, we all can move?
Then they said : The earth belongs to the living,
We refuse allegiance, we resign office, and we love.

They are writing at their desks, the thinking fathers,
They do not recognize their live sons' faces;
Slave and slaveholder they are chained together
And one is ancestor and one is child.
Escape the birthplace; walk into the world
Refusing to be either slave or slaveholder.

WHEREVER

Wherever
we walk
we will make

Wherever
we protest
we will go planting

Make poems
seed grass
feed a child growing
build a house
Whatever we stand against
We will stand feeding and seeding

Wherever
I walk
I will make

FLYING TO HANOI

I thought I was going to the poets, but I am
    going to the children.
I thought I was going to the children, but I am
    going to the women.
I thought I was going to the women, but I am going
    to the fighters.
I thought I was going to the fighters, but I am going
    to the men and women who are inventing peace.
I thought I was going to the inventors of peace,
    but I am going to the poets.
My life is flying to your life.

HOW WE DID IT

We all traveled into that big room,
some from very far away
we smiled at some we knew
we did not as we talked agree
our hearts went fast thinking of morning
when we would walk along the path.
We spoke.   Late night.   We disagreed.
We knew we would climb the Senate steps.
We knew we would present our claim
we would demand : be strong now : end the war.
How would we do it?   What would we ask?
"We will be warned," one said. "They will warn us and take us."
"We can speak and walk away."
"We can lie down as if in mourning."
"We can lie down as a way of speech,
speaking of all the dead in Asia."
Then Eqbal said, "We are not at this moment
a revolutionary group, we are
a group of dissenters.   Let some, then,
walk away, let some stand until they want to leave,
let some lie down and let some be arrested.   Some of us.
Let each do what he feels at that moment

tomorrow." Eqbal's dark face.
The doctor spoke, of friendships made in jail.
We looked into each other's eyes
and went all to our rooms, to sleep,
waiting for morning.

ISLANDS

O for God's sake
they are connected
underneath

They look at each other
across the glittering sea
some keep a low profile

Some are cliffs
The bathers think
islands are separate like them

RESURRECTION OF THE RIGHT SIDE

When the half-body dies its frightful death
forked pain, infection of snakes, lightning, pull down the
    voice.   Waking
and I begin to climb the mountain on my mouth,
word by stammer, walk stammered, the lurching deck of earth.
Left-right with none of my own rhythms
the long-established sex and poetry.
                                  I go running in sleep,
but waking stumble down corridors of self, all rhythms gone.

The broken movement of love   sex out of rhythm
one halted name   in a shattered language
ruin of French-blue lights behind the eyes
slowly the left hand extends a hundred feet
and the right hand follows follows
but still the power of sight is very weak
but I go rolling this ball of life, it rolls
and I follow it whole up the slowly-brightening slope

A whisper attempts me, I whisper without stammer
I walk the long hall to the time of a metronome

set by a child's gun-target   left-right
the power of eyesight is very slowly arriving
in this late impossible daybreak
all the blue flowers open

POEM   WHITE PAGE   WHITE PAGE   POEM

Poem   white page   white page   poem
something is streaming out of a body in waves
something is beginning from the fingertips
they are starting to declare for my whole life
all the despair and the making music
something like wave after wave
that breaks on a beach
something like bringing the entire life
to this moment
the small waves bringing themselves to white paper
something like light stands up and is alive

BEFORE DANGER

There were poems all over Broadway that morning.
Blowing across traffic.   Against the legs.
Held for a moment on the backs of hands.
Drifts of poems in doorways.
The crowd was a river to the highest tower
all the way down that avenue.
Snow on that river, torn paper
of their faces.

Late at night, in a dark-blue sleep,
the paper stopped blowing.
Lightning struck at me from behind my eyes.

RECOVERING

Dream of the world
speaking to me.

The dream of the dead
acted out in me.

The fathers shouting
across their blue gulf.

A storm in each word,
an incomplete universe.

Lightning in brain,
slow-time recovery.

In the light of October
things emerge clear.

The force of looking
returns to my eyes.

Darkness arrives
splitting the mind open.

Something again
is beginning to be born.

A dance is
dancing me.

I wake in the dark.

THE GATES

Scaffolding.   *A poet is in solitary; the expectation is that he will be*
tried and summarily executed on a certain day in autumn. He has been
on this cycle before : condemned to death, the sentence changed to life
imprisonment, and then a pardon from his President during a time of
many arrests and executions, a time of terror. The poet has written his
stinging work—like that of Burns or Brecht—and it has got under the
skin of the highest officials. He is Kim Chi Ha.
An American woman is sent to make an appeal for the poet's life. She
speaks to Cabinet ministers, the Cardinal, university people, writers,
the poet's family and his infant son. She stands in the mud and rain at
the prison gates—also the gates of perception, the gates of the body. She
is before the house of the poet. He is in solitary.

1

Waiting to leave all day I hear the words;
That poet in prison, that poet newly-died
whose words we wear, reading, all of us.   I and my son.

All day we read the words:
friends, lovers, daughters, grandson,
and all night the distant loves
and I who had never seen him am drawn to him

Through acts, through poems,
through our closenesses—
whatever links us in our variousness;
across worlds, love and poems and justices
wishing to be born.

2

Walking the world to find the poet of these cries.
But this walking is flying the streets of all the air.

Walking the world, through the people at airports,
this city of hills, this island ocean fire-blue and now this city.

Walking this world is driving the roads of houses
endless tiles   houses, fast streams, now this child's house.

Walking under the sharp mountains through the sharp city
circled in time by rulers, their grip; the marvelous
hard-gripped people silent among their rulers, looking at me.

3 New Friends

The new friend comes into my hotel room
smiling.   He does a curious thing.
He walks around the room, touching
all the pictures hanging on the wall.
One picture does not move.

A new friend assures me : Foreigners are safe,
You speak for writers, you are safe, he says.
There will be no car
driving up behind you, there will be
no accident, he says.   I know these accidents.
Nothing will follow you, he says.
O the Mafia at home, I know, Black Hand
of childhood, the death of Tresca whom I mourn,
the building of New York.   Many I know.
This morning I go early to see the Cardinal.
When I return, the new friend is waiting.   His face
wax-candle-pool-color, he saying
"I thought you were kidnapped."

A missionary comes to visit me.
Looks into my eyes.   Says,
"Turn on the music so we can talk."

4

The Cabinet minister speaks of liberation.
"Do you know how the Communists use this word?"
We all use the word.   Liberation.

No, but look—these are his diaries,
says the Cabinet minister.
These were found in the house of the poet.
Look, Liberation, Liberation, he is speaking in praise.

He says, this poet, It is not wrong
to take from the rich and give to the poor.

Yes.   He says it in prose speech, he says it in his plays,
he says it in his poems that bind me to him,
that bind his people and mine in these new ways
for the first time past strangeness and despisal.

It also means that you broke into his house and stole his papers.

5

Among the days,
among the nights of the poet in solitary,

a strong infant is just beginning to run.
I go up the stepping-stones
to where the young wife of the poet
stands holding the infant in her arms.
She weeps, she weeps.
But the poet's son looks at me
and the wife's mother looks at me with a keen look
across her grief.   Lights in the house, books making every wall
a wall of speech.
                              The clasp of the woman's hand
around my wrist, a keen band
more steel than the words
Save his life.

I feel that clasp on my bones.

A strong infant is beginning to run.

6 The Church of Galilee

As we climb to the church of Galilee
Three harsh men on the corner.
As we go to the worship-meeting of the dismissed,
three state police on the street.
As we all join at the place of the dispossessed,

three dark men asking their rote questions.
As we go ahead to stand with our new friends
that will be our friends our lifetime.
Introduced as dismissed from this faculty, this college,
this faculty, this university.
'Dismissed' is now an honorary degree.
The harsh police are everywhere,
they have hunted this fellowship away before
and they are everywhere, at the street-corner,
listening to all hymns,
standing before all doors,
hearing over all wires.
We go up to Galilee.
Let them listen to the dispossessed
and to all women and men who stand firm and sing
wanting a shared and honest lifetime.
Let them listen to Galilee.

7 The Dream of Galilee

That night, a flute
across the dark, the sound
opening times to me, a time
when I stood on the green hillside
before the great white stone.

Grave of my ancestor
Akiba at rest over Kinneret.
The holy poem, he said to me,
the Song of Songs always;
and know what I know, to love
your belief with all your life,
and resist the Romans, as I did,
even to the torture and beyond.
Over Kinneret, with all of them,
Jesus, all the Judeans,
that other Galilee
in dream across war I see.

8 Mother as Pitchfork

Woman seen as a slender instrument,
woman at vigil in the prison-yard,
woman seen as the fine tines of a pitchfork
that works hard, that is worn down, rusted down
to a fine sculpture standing in a yard
where her son's body is confined.
Woman as fine tines blazing against sunset,
wavering lines against yellow brightness
where her fine body becomes transparent in bravery,
where she will live and die as the tines of a pitchfork

that stands to us as her son's voice does stand
across the world speaking

The rumor comes that if this son is killed
this mother will kill herself

But she is here, she lives,
the slender tines of this pitchfork standing in flames of light.

9

You grief woman   you gave me a scarlet coverlet
thick-sown with all the flowers
and all the while your poet sleeps in stone

Grief woman, the waves of this coverlet,
roses of Asia,
they flicker soft and bright over my sleep

all night while the poet waits in solitary

All you vigil women, I start up in the night,
fling back this cover of red;
in long despair we work   write   speak   pray   call to others
Free our night   free our lives   free our poet

10

Air fills with fear and the kinds of fear:

The fear of the child among the tyrannical
unanswerable men and women, they dominate day and night.

Fear of the young lover in the huge rejection
ambush of sex and imagination;
fear that the world will not allow your work.

Fear of the overarching wars and poverties,
the terrible exiles,
all bound by corruption until at last!   we speak!

And those at home in jail who protest the frightful war
and the beginning : The woman-guard says to me, Spread your cheeks,
the search begins and I begin to know.

And also at home the nameless multitude
of fears : fear in childbirth for the living child,
fear for the child deformed and loved, fear
among the surgeries that can cure her, fear
for the child's father, and for oneself, fear.
Fear of the cunt and cock in their terrible powers

and here a world away fear of the jailers' tortures
for we invent our fear and act it out
in ripping, in burning, in blood, in the terrible scream
and in tearing away every mouth that screams.

Giant fears : massacres, the butchered that across the fields of the world
lie screaming, and their screams are heard as silence.
O love, knowing your love across a world of fear,
I lie in a strange country, in pale yellow, swamp-green, woods
and a night of music while a poet lies in solitary
somewhere in a concrete cell.   Glare-lit, I hear,
without books, without pen and paper.
Does he draw a pencil out of his throat,
out of his veins, out of his sex?
There are cells all around him, emptied.
He can signal on these walls till he runs mad.
He is signalling to me across the night.

He is signalling.   Many of us speak,
we do teach each other, we do act through our fears.

Where is the world that will touch life to this prison?

We run through the night.   We are given his gifts.

11

Long ago, soon after my son's birth
—this scene comes in arousal with the sight of a strong child
just beginning to run—
when all life seemed prisoned off, because the father's other son
born three weeks before my child
had opened the world
that other son and his father closed the world—
in my fierce loneliness and fine well-being
torn apart but with my amazing child
I celebrated and grieved.
And before that baby
had ever started to begin to run
then Mary said,
smiling and looking out of her Irish eyes,
"Never mind, Muriel.
Life will come will come again
knocking and coughing and farting at your door."

12

For that I cannot name the names,
my child's own father, the flashing, the horseman,

the son of the poet—
for that he never told me another child was started,
to come to birth three weeks before my own.
Tragic timing that sets the hands of time.
O wind from our own coast, turning
around the turning world.

Wind from the continents, this other child,
child of this moment and this moment's poet.
Again I am struck nameless, unable to name,
and the axe-blows fall heavy heavy and sharp
and the moon strikes his white light down over the continents
on this strong infant and the heroic friends
silent in this terrifying moment under all moonlight,
all sunlight turning in all our unfree lands.
Name them, name them all, light of our own time.

13

Crucified child—is he crucified?   he is tortured,
kept away from his father, spiked on time,
crucified we say, cut off from the man
they want to kill—
he runs toward me in Asia, crying.
Flash gives me my own son strong and those years ago

cut off from his own father and running toward me
holding a strong flower.

Child of this moment, you are your father's child
wherever your father is prisoned, by what tyrannies
or jailed as my child's father
by his own fantasies—
child of the age running among the world,
standing among us who carry our own time.

14

So I became very dark very large
a silent woman this time given to speech
a woman of the river   of that song
and on the beach of the world in storm given
in long lightning seeing the rhyming of those scenes
that make our lives.
Anne Sexton the poet saying
ten days ago to that receptive friend,
the friend of the hand-held camera:
"Muriel is serene."
Am I that in their sight?
Word comes today of Anne's
of Anne's long-approaching

of Anne's over-riding over-falling
suicide.   Speak for   sing for   pray for
everyone in solitary
every living life.

15

All day the rain
all day waiting within the prison gate
before another prison gate
The house of the poet
He is in there somewhere
among the muscular wardens
I have arrived at the house of the poet
in the mud in the interior music of all poems
and the grey rain of the world
whose gates do not open.
I stand, and for this religion and that religion
do not eat but remember all the things I know
and a strong infant beginning to run.
Nothing is happening.   Mud, silence, rain.

Near the end of the day
with the rain and the knowledge pulling at my legs
a movement behind me makes me move aside.

A bus full of people turns in the mud, drives to the gate.
The gate that never opens
opens at last.   Beyond it, slender
Chinese-red posts of the inner gates.
The gate of the house of the poet.

The bus is crowded, a rush-hour bus that waits.
Nobody moves.

"Who are these people?" I say.
How can these gates open?

My new friend has run up beside me.
He has been standing guard in the far corner.
"They are prisoners," he says, "brought here from trial.
Don't you see?   They are all tied together."

Fool that I am!   I had not seen the ropes,
down at their wrists in the crowded rush-hour bus.

The gates are open.   The prisoners go in.
The house of the poet who stays in solitary,
not allowed reading   not allowed writing
not allowed   his woman   his friends   his unknown friends
and the strong infant beginning to run.

We go down the prison hill.   On our right, sheds
full of people all leaning forward, blown on some ferry.
"They are the families of the prisoners.   Some can visit.
They are waiting for their numbers to be called."

How shall we venture home?
How shall we tell each other of the poet?
How can we meet the judgment on the poet,
or his execution?   How shall we free him?
How shall we speak to the infant beginning to run?
All those beginning to run?